LAW OF THE SEA

LAW OF THE SEA

U.S. Policy Dilemma

Edited by

BERNARD H. OXMAN
DAVID D. CARON
CHARLES L. O. BUDERI

ICS PRESS

Institute for Contemporary Studies
San Francisco, California

Inquiries, book orders, and catalog requests should be addressed to ICS Press, Suite 811, 260 California Street, San Francisco, California 94111—415—398—3010.

Library of Congress Cataloging in Publication Data
Main entry under title:

Law of the sea

    Includes bibliographical references and index.
    1. Maritime law. I. Oxman, Bernard H. II. Caron,
David D. III. Buderi, Charles L. O.
JX4411.L37 1983   341.4'5   83—10788
ISBN 0—917616—59—6
ISBN 0—917616—53—7 (pbk.)

CONTENTS

III
Practical Differences: Seabed Mining

V
Appendix

PREFACE

After a decade of negotiation, the Third United Nations Conference on the Law of the Sea produced a treaty to deal comprehensively with the use of the ocean and the resources in and under it. More than 120 countries have signed the treaty. The United States and several other highly industrialized nations have thus far refused, finding the provisions governing the exploitation of undersea minerals to be no more than a thinly disguised scheme for some countries—or their rulers—to expropriate wealth and technology belonging to others.

The Reagan administration's decision to stay outside of the treaty and to rely instead on customary law and "mini-treaties" was controversial. The larger treaty had raised fundamental questions of politics and economics—questions of private property rights, of the meaning and effect of sovereignty, of the purpose and nature of international law itself.

This book reflects and tries to illuminate the controversy. Many of the authors participated in the treaty negotiations. Many also participated in two conferences on the law of the sea that significantly influenced the spirited debate presented here. The first conference, "Perspectives on U.S. Policy toward the Law of the Sea," was held at the Boalt Hall Law School of the University of California, Berkeley, in February 1982 and was sponsored by the Boalt Hall International Law Society, the American Society of International Law, and the Earl Warren Legal Institute. The second conference, "U.S. Law of the Sea Policy: Options for the Future," organized by the Center for Oceans Law and Policy of the University of Virginia School of Law, was held in Montego Bay, Jamaica, in January 1983—a month after the Law of the Sea Treaty was opened for signature—and offered further perspectives on the reasoning of the Reagan administration. We thank the conference organizers and the Institute's National Public Policy Fellows, Mr. Robert Kiernan and Mr. Bruce Pencek, for their assistance in the publication of this volume.

The roles and mutual relation of national and international law in economic and political affairs were key issues surrounding the Law of the Sea Treaty. They also have figured prominently in other books published by the Institute for Contemporary Studies, notably *The Third World: Premises of U.S. Policy,* edited by W. Scott Thompson and just recently revised, and a forthcoming study of world economic growth problems edited by Professor Arnold Harberger.

Glenn Dumke
President
Institute for Contemporary Studies

I

Introduction

1

DAVID D. CARON

Reconciling Domestic Principles and International Cooperation

Since the early part of this century it has grown increasingly apparent that the traditional international law of the sea has become inadequate to deal with the ever-greater demands being placed on the world's oceans. For example, it became clear that management of rapidly diminishing fish stocks in some regions could not simply be left to each country. Similarly, increasing technical capabilities created new questions as to who owned the oil of the continental shelf and the minerals of the deep seabed. As coastal states considered gaining control of fisheries and offshore minerals by extending their ocean jurisdiction, the possibility arose that traditional notions of free navigation might be jeopardized. Following a series of important but unsuccessful attempts to

create a new legal order,[1] the United Nations General Assembly in
1970 decided to convene a Third United Nations Conference on
the Law of the Sea (UNCLOS III) to address the exploitation of the
deep seabed and the "broad range of related issues."

The opening session of the conference was held in Caracas during the summer of 1974. The range of ocean interests considered
by the conference had never been the subject of a single treaty.
Because the conference addressed all the issues simultaneously
and because the negotiating nations had different interests and
intentions, the give-and-take quickly lent the treaty the aspect of
a package deal. Despite disagreements requiring compromise, the
general outline of a treaty on all but the deep seabed issues
emerged so quickly at the first session that two of the U.S. representatives wrote that there could be "a widely acceptable Law of
the Sea Treaty in 1975."[2]

Because of the unresolved deep seabed issues, however, this pre-
diction turned out to be optimistic. Negotiating positions initially
were polarized over the amount of international control that
should be present in a deep seabed regime. Most developed nations, including the United States, argued for a simple international registry for deep seabed claims. Developing states, on the
other hand, pressed for the creation of an international "Enterprise" that would have the sole authority to pursue exploitation
of the deep seabed. As a compromise in 1976, then Secretary of
State Henry Kissinger proposed a "parallel system" that created
an international Enterprise while assuring access to the deep
seabed for state and private mining efforts.[3]

Having agreed to a framework of relatively high suprana-
tionality, negotiators shifted the focus of their efforts to the
framework in which such supranational power would be exercised,
the International Seabed Authority.[4] In its fifth through ninth
sessions, the conference negotiated the details of this parallel
system for development of the deep seabed. Great progress was
made at the ninth session in 1980, and the conference adjourned
looking forward to completing the final text in 1981.[5] Criticism of
the treaty within the United States had begun to mount, however.

Evolution of Criticism within the United States

From the beginning, congressional reaction to developments in the law of the sea was mixed.[6] When Arvid Pardo proposed to the United Nations in 1967 that an international agency act as a trustee over the seabed for all states, many members of Congress argued that the United Nations was not mature enough to handle such a task.[7] American disillusionment and frustration with the UN was easily transferred to the proposed and somewhat similarly structured International Seabed Authority and was generally a consistent undercurrent in the criticism of the treaty. In this vein, Northcutt Ely's view of the law of the sea negotiations echoed then Ambassador Daniel P. Moynihan's comments on the UN: America was "endorsing principles for whose logical outcome it was wholly unprepared and with which it could never actually go along." Ely agreed with Moynihan that "these days the United Nations [and UNCLOS III] often takes on the appearance of an international court with the Third World pressing the charges and conducting a trial." In what would become characteristic of the political fervor of the treaty's opponents, he also accepted Moynihan's conclusion: "What then does the United States do? The United States goes into opposition."[8]

Criticism of the treaty generally took one of two forms. One approach examined the many ocean interests of the United States (notably in fisheries, mineral resources, navigation, and national security) and weighed the loss or gain for the U.S. from the UNCLOS III package deal. Although there is disagreement about the overall impact of the treaty on American ocean interests, particularly in the controversial area of deep seabed mining, many commentators would argue that U.S. ocean interests on the whole are advanced by the treaty. Many others would argue that, regardless of overall impact, the weighing of substantial interests is not currently the most pressing area of debate over the treaty.

This leads to the second line of criticism, which concerns itself with the precedential effect of the convention on systems of world governance and theories of international economic relations. The debate focuses particularly on the convention's treatment of deep seabed mining and compulsory dispute settlement—the areas in which the convention takes unprecedented steps toward suprana-

tionality. This broader concern has been the prime force behind
the U.S. rejection of the treaty.

Dangerous precedents have been seen in many parts of the Law
of the Sea Treaty. In particular, production limitations, mandatory
transfer of some technologies, and an apparent built-in preference
for public over private enterprise have been viewed as precedents
that could be turned against American economic interests.[9]

These concerns were aggravated during the 1970s by the energy
crisis and by the growing demand of the Third World for a global
rearrangement of economic relations under a "New International
Economic Order" (NIEO).[10] Fearing adverse effects on competition, private investment, and future economic growth, opponents
of the treaty and of the NIEO debated the implications of the
transfer and socialization of technology. They also disapproved of
the virtual absence of U.S. affirmative power in the proposed
organization of the Seabed Authority. In addition, they speculated
that the treaty's limits on production and its failure to assure U.S.
access to strategic minerals might increase American dependence
on hostile foreign sources.

Despite all these expressions of disapproval within the United
States, the conference believed in 1981 that negotiation of the
treaty was virtually concluded. This difference between U.S. attitudes at home and the position taken by U.S. negotiators at the
conference existed in large part because of the domestic structure
of American foreign policy making. Under the Constitution, the
Senate must approve treaties negotiated by the executive branch,
judging whether the benefits of ratification outweigh the costs of
reaching agreement. As the ninth session of the conference ended,
however, the executive and the Senate possessed quite different
views as to the acceptability of the convention. In part this occurred because the executive branch, through three administrations, had been intimately involved with the negotiations and the
compromises leading to the "package deal." Meanwhile, the primary involvement of the Senate as an institution had been through
its prolonged consideration of a domestic law to regulate deep
seabed mining proposed by American interest groups critical of
the convention. With the tempests surrounding the Panama
Canal and SALT II treaties fresh in mind, observers thought that
any battle for acceptance of the convention would be waged in the

Senate and not in the executive branch. It was thought possible, if not certain, that the Senate would withhold its advice and consent.

The election of President Reagan changed this institutional context entirely. Thoroughly agreeing with the precedential concerns of the Senate, the Reagan administration moved these areas of concern back into the negotiations themselves. On 2 March 1981, shortly after the Reagan administration took office, the Department of State announced that it would "seek to ensure that the negotiations do not end at the present session of the conference, pending a policy review by the United States government."[11] Third World representatives expressed "disbelief and consternation" that the premises of negotiation should be reexamined at the end of a decade of effort and compromise.[12]

Despite Third World charges of bad faith, the U.S. negotiators successfully ensured that the negotiations did not end at the tenth session of the conference in August 1981. The results of the U.S. policy review were announced by President Reagan on 29 January 1982. The president stated that the U.S. would return to the negotiations and work with other countries to achieve an acceptable treaty. The president's statement went on to outline six objectives that the U.S. delegation would seek in the eleventh session, objectives generally addressing the precedents described above. Although changes to the draft convention were agreed to at the eleventh session, the United States concluded that it would not join in the general adoption of the text.

At the official opening of the treaty for signature in Jamaica on 10 December 1982, 117 nations signed the convention. The great bulk of these signatories were developing countries. It is important to note, however, that a group of Western developed countries (including Australia, Canada, Denmark, France, Greece, Ireland, the Netherlands, Norway, and Sweden) and the majority of the Socialist nations (including the Soviet Union, several Eastern European countries, and China) were also original signatories. Belgium, the Federal Republic of Germany, Italy, and the United Kingdom joined the United States in not signing the convention because of concerns over the deep seabed mining provisions. Approximately a score of other nations did not sign, for reasons of their own. Four more nations, including Japan, have signed the treaty since December.

Concerns of Principle — The Decisive Question

The United States did not sign the Law of the Sea Convention because the treaty was perceived as a threat to basic principles of Western economic and political philosophy. Tragically, the treaty could not simply be renegotiated, because the concerns of the United States went to the basic premises upon which years of compromise and negotiation had been built. Whether the U.S. negotiators had gained a treaty satisfying the immediate and direct American interests in fisheries or commercial and military navigation was not the decisive question for the Reagan administration. Rather, the symbolic and long-term implications of the precedents set by the treaty were the major forces shaping U.S. policy. These concerns will dominate American policy toward the law of the sea for many years to come. The precedential concerns will be central to future executive or congressional considerations of joining the treaty and of supporting alternatives to the UN Convention on the Law of the Sea. The role and value of U.S. concerns of principle, specifically in the law of the sea and generally in all international cooperation, is the subject of this book.

Part II provides a sampling of the political spectrum of opinion on the value and implications for world order of the convention's deep seabed mining regime. Arvid Pardo, in direct opposition to the present U.S. administration, criticizes the convention, not because it went too far, but rather because it did not go far enough and thereby failed to seize the opportunities offered. Pardo argues that a world whose stability and health are fragile in many ways requires international cooperation on unprecedented levels, and that cooperation will require that some national principles, like some national practical interests, be subordinated. Given the existence of the Law of the Sea Convention, it must further be asked in what areas and to what degrees a nation's substantive practical interests should be sacrificed in the defense of certain principles. Leigh Ratiner and W. Scott Burke and Frank Brokaw in separate essays examine whether overall the interests of the United States are better served by working within the convention's framework or by seeking an alternative regime. Finally, across the spectrum from Professor Pardo, Robert Goldwin argues that the treaty's deep seabed regime not only institutionalizes a set of principles contrary to American economic and political philosophy but also hinders the achievement of a world order that respects the real common heritage of mankind.

Returning to American practical interests in the deep seabed, part III examines more fully the details of the possible deep seabed regimes. Lance Antrim and James Sebenius explore the incentives that will be created for ocean mining under the convention, while Lewis Cohen considers the possibility of mining under coordinated national regimes—the "mini-treaty" option.

Bringing together these discussions, part IV focuses on future American law of the sea policy and the implications that policy will have for international order. Joseph Nye examines the political implications of accepting or rejecting the treaty. Bernard Oxman considers the role and value of principle, the actual threat posed to American principles by the treaty, and how the U.S. and the international community must deal with such concerns of principle in the attempt to build a law of the sea.

Professor Pardo's observation that the world condition demands international cooperation on unprecedented levels cannot be readily denied. In fact, the older model of international law as a system of mutual national self-restraint is already giving way to one based on positive cooperation. This trend raises the question of how best to reconcile the political and economic sovereignty of individual countries with the need for supranational responses to some problems. The ways nations achieve this difficult balance will almost certainly turn on the weight they accord their domestic principles of political and economic justice. The stakes are very high. The law of the sea is only one expression of this far broader concern that embraces such other issues as the international allocation of valuable earth orbits, the international regulation of the press, and the United Nations itself.

American rejection of the Law of the Sea Convention has grave implications that should not be easily discounted. The treaty contains innovative provisions long sought by the U.S. for compulsory international settlement of disputes. It also, through its promotion of common expectations as to the rights of nations, offers the possibility of reducing needless conflicts and tensions at sea. The decision nonetheless to reject the treaty flowed from the perception that it was contrary to basic American beliefs. That such a fundamental disagreement could exist after the most extensive negotiations in history suggests more than a mere failure of the conference. It suggests institutional problems in the formation of American policy and an underlying division of opinion within the United States as to the most appropriate policy. Most significantly, such a fundamental disagreement suggests a tremendous rift in the international community itself in the area of international economic relations. Cicero once wrote that it is the existence of a community that allows the creation of law and that, conversely, if there is no community, there can be no law.[13] To the degree that building an international law of cooperation requires a philosophical consensus in the international community, there must be careful study of the role and value nations give their own principles.

II

*Rights, Interests, and
International Equity*

2

ARVID PARDO

An Opportunity Lost

The increasing value of ocean space is bringing about the demise of traditional law of the sea. Like Humpty-Dumpty, all the king's horses and all the king's men cannot put traditional law of the sea together again. They cannot because traditional law of the sea, which served the international community so well for more than three centuries, cannot readily be adapted to a situation where ocean space and its resources are being used and exploited ever more intensely.

The recently concluded law of the sea negotiations also have another aspect: they are—together with questions of disarmament, the New International Economic Order, and others—a part of the contemporary global *problematique* of peace. They are influenced by and in turn influence negotiations in other areas of the *problematique*.

This chapter is a revised version of a paper presented at the Duke University School of Law symposium on the law of the sea, 28 and 29 October 1982. Copyright© 1983, *Law and Contemporary Problems*.

We must understand these basic facts in order intelligently to evaluate the historic convention[1] adopted by the Third United Nations Conference on the Law of the Sea (UNCLOS III) last year, the preparation of which was a major achievement in itself.

The treaty's important innovations are almost too numerous to list. They include:

- the concept of transit passage through straits used for international navigation;

- the concept of archipelagic baselines and archipelagic waters;

- the concept of the exclusive economic zone;

- fundamental change in the definition of the legal continental shelf;

- explicit recognition of scientific research and construction of artificial islands and other installations as freedoms of the high seas;

- the duty of international cooperation in the development and transfer of marine science and technology;

- the concept of a comprehensive environmental law of the sea based on the obligation of all states to protect and preserve the marine environment.

These provisions among many others, some technical and some substantive, are complemented by two far-reaching innovations that, if effectively implemented, could mark a revolution not merely in the law of the sea but in international relations. I refer to the dispute settlement system, which is the most comprehensive, flexible, and binding system of its kind devised up to now by the international community, and to the international agreement that the seabed and its mineral resources beyond the limits of national jurisdiction have a special legal status as the common heritage of mankind. The establishment of an effective international organization to implement this principle could be a precedent of incalculable importance for the future.

Inevitably a complex document, such as this 200-page convention, that deals with highly controversial matters involving vital interests of states cannot be expected to be without shortcomings. The important question, however, is not whether the convention has shortcomings but whether these more than counterbalance its positive aspects.

From the point of view of world order, the major concern must be whether the present convention adequately serves the functions that all international law must serve, i.e., (a) accommodation of interests, (b) prevention of conflict, (c) predictability, and (d) promotion of common or community objectives.

Accommodation of Interests

We are all aware of the framework within which the Law of the Sea Conference was held—the vital military importance of ocean space, the fact that ocean space contains incalculable living and nonliving resources, the importance of navigation and other uses of the sea—and we are all aware that traditional uses of the sea are being radically transformed by technology, and that new, varied, and important uses are arising.

The convention obviously bears throughout the mark of accommodation of interests, for without such accommodation it would have been impossible to elaborate a text that has been signed by the great majority of states. It could even be argued that accommodation in some cases may have been carried too far. Thus certain important provisions, such as Article 7 (2) and the last sentence in Article 47 (7), have been inserted in the convention merely to accommodate the interests of a single state. The question is not whether accommodation of interests and political compromise—the so-called "package deal" so long and tenaciously pursued at the conference—were necessary, but whether apparent political compromises in the convention are substantive or only carefully drafted formulations designed to mask continued fundamental disagreement on basic issues. In this case, of course, no real accommodation of interests has occurred and conflict is not avoided but merely postponed.

It is impossible to generalize in this connection. In some cases, for instance, with respect to the limits of the territorial sea, the provisions of the convention undoubtedly reflect substantive agreement on the part of the overwhelming majority of the international community. In other, far more numerous instances, however, there are strong grounds for believing that representa-

tives at the conference, having ascertained the difficulty of reaching agreement on the substance of an issue, thereafter searched
mainly for a formula sufficiently vague or sufficiently ambiguous
to permit all significant states concerned to claim that their policy
objectives had been more or less satisfactorily achieved. Thus Article 76 of the convention on the definition of the so-called "continental shelf"—a term that now bears little relationship to its original meaning—enables states that argued for a clearly defined
maximum limit of the shelf to claim that such a limit has been incorporated in the convention.[2] At the same time, those states that
argued for an expansive, flexible definition of the legal continental
shelf are reasonably satisfied, for they are aware that baselines
are established at the discretion of the coastal state within the
broad guidelines of Article 7, that the wording of Article 76 is
sufficiently flexible and ambiguous to accommodate most coastal
state claims, and that the proposed Commission on the Limits of
the Continental Shelf has only powers of recommendation. Article
74 on the delimitation of the exclusive economic zone between
states with opposite or adjacent coasts is another example of a
formula designed to satisfy the requirements of states with
diametrically opposed views. A further example is the phrase "exclusively for peaceful purposes," which recurs with a certain fre-
quency in the convention. The meaning of the phrase is nowhere
defined, but the words convey the vague, misleading, but useful
impression that somehow the ongoing intensive militarization of
ocean space is being reversed. Those states that wish strictly to
limit the military uses of ocean space can claim that the arms race
in the seas has been significantly limited, while those states that
consider extensive military use of the seas a regrettable necessity
are not incommodated. Several further provisions of this kind
could be cited.

Silence, Ambiguity, and Unpredictability

Vagueness, ambiguity, and sometimes silence on major questions
do not further achievement of two additional objectives: prevention of conflict and predictability, i.e., the ability to foresee what
activities can be undertaken with reasonable assurance that other
states will acquiesce. It is difficult to assert that the convention

performs this latter function consistently. The convention, of course, is very clear on the fact that all economic uses of the marine environment are reserved to coastal states *at least* to 200 nautical miles from the appropriate baselines. It is also true that the rights of coastal states are in general carefully outlined, particularly within the exclusive economic zone and the legal continental shelf. However, when the convention deals with matters other than the rights of coastal states, it is often studiously unclear, and predictability suffers.

For example, Article 19 purports to give objective definition to the principle of innocent passage of foreign vessels in the territorial sea. Passage of a foreign ship is considered prejudicial to the peace, good order, or security of a coastal state, and hence not innocent, if it engages in any one of a dozen or so enumerated activities including "any activity not having a direct bearing on passage." But Article 19 does *not* state that a foreign ship *not* engaging in the enumerated activities has the right of innocent passage. Thus the right of innocent passage remains subject to the discretion of the coastal state concerned. Part III of the convention establishes the right of transit passage through "straits used for international navigation between one part of the high seas or an exclusive economic zone and another part of the high seas or an exclusive economic zone," but the term "straits used for international navigation" is not clearly defined. The English Channel and the Strait of Gibraltar, through which hundreds of ships pass daily, are clearly straits used for international navigation, but the legal status of many less frequently transited straits could be doubtful. Indeed even the legal status of heavily used straits may be contested.[3] It is surprising that the drafters of the convention did not take the opportunity to clarify the legal status of many straits by adding an annex to the convention enumerating those straits that are considered to be used for international navigation, as has been done for living resources of the sea considered highly migratory. It also would have been useful to include in the convention an article providing for compulsory and binding settlement of disputes over whether a particular strait is used for international navigation.

Silence is another technique that has been used to avoid mention of controversial problems. Thus there is no mention in the convention of any of the numerous outstanding legal issues concerning the Arctic and Antarctic. Far more important, the convention ignores the many issues relating to military uses of the marine environment. While most powers go to considerable lengths to avoid confrontations in the seas, one can anticipate that certain legally doubtful military uses of the marine environment could give rise to dangerous incidents in the present international climate. Certainly the question of military uses of the seas is highly delicate, and perhaps one should not expect the convention to contain mandatory provisions on this subject. Nonetheless it is unfortunate that on this vital matter the convention provides no guidance whatsoever. It contains a vast number of recommendations and exhortations on a variety of subjects of varying importance. It would have been useful had it something to say on a subject that could involve the peace of the world.[4]

Promotion of Community Objectives

A comprehensive law of the sea treaty should promote common or community objectives, such as the protection of the marine environment. Part XII of the convention, the remarkable work of Committee III of the conference, significantly develops international law in this connection. Nevertheless even in this portion of the text—which in many respects is unique—there are serious deficiencies, including complete silence on the controversial question of the disposal of radioactive wastes. This is a question that was singled out for special mention in the 1958 Geneva Convention on the High Seas,[5] and it is a matter of more than ordinary importance now when the use of nuclear energy for peaceful purposes is spreading throughout the world and the seabed is being seriously considered as a possible permanent waste disposal site by an increasing number of countries.

In this connection it may be worthwhile to observe that substantial quantities of low-level radioactive wastes have been dumped in the sea since 1946, often with few precautions; it would also appear that high-level radioactive wastes occasionally have been deposited on the seabed. For a number of reasons, including the accumulation of high-level radioactive wastes on temporary sites on land, seabed or subseabed disposal of such wastes is being increasingly studied. While radioactive wastes no doubt may be one of the "toxic, harmful, or noxious substances" mentioned in Article 194 (3) (a) of the convention, and while it is true that under Article 210 (1) states have accepted the obligation to "adopt laws and regulations to prevent, reduce, and control pollution of the marine environment by dumping," nevertheless it seems highly unfortunate that the drafters of the present convention did not see fit to single out the dumping or release of radioactive wastes in the marine environment as worthy of special precautions. It is unlikely that this mission is fortuitous, since the convention contains special provisions (Article 23) on foreign nuclear-powered ships transiting the territorial sea.

Equity

It is perhaps fair to conclude, from a non-national point of view, that the convention, because of its silence, vagueness, or ambiguity on many fundamental questions, does not consistently serve any of the functions that all international law must serve.

The convention should not be evaluated in isolation, however. A treaty of limited value in itself could be extremely valuable if it were to strengthen world order by furthering equity between states or by suggesting effective solutions to resource management and conservation problems in the marine environment.

As far as equity is concerned, there can be no doubt that the convention, far from furthering equity between states, reflects primarily the highly acquisitive instincts of many coastal states, both developed and developing, particularly of states with long coastlines fronting upon the open oceans. The magnitude of this appropriation, which has been carried out under a cloud of misleading rhetoric, is unprecedented in history.

Probably more than 40 percent of ocean space, by far the most valuable in terms of economic uses and accessible resources, is placed under some form of national control. All known commercially exploitable hydrocarbon deposits, all commercially exploitable minerals in unconsolidated sediments from sand and gravel to tin, most phosphorite nodule deposits, a significant portion of the recently discovered polymetallic sulphide and cobalt crust deposits, several manganese nodule deposits, over 90 percent of commercially exploited living resources of the sea, and all known sites suitable for the production of energy from the sea, are all now recognized as the exclusive property of coastal states.

Nor is this all. Since the limits of national jurisdiction are not clearly defined in the convention, some coastal states fronting on the open sea and some mid-ocean archipelagos can continue, within certain limits, to extend their control in the marine environment as their marine capabilities increase or as their national interests appear to dictate.

Despite timid attempts at compensation, it is impossible to deny that the convention is grossly inequitable not only to landlocked and geographically disadvantaged states but also to most coastal states themselves. According to some knowledgeable persons, only a dozen or so coastal states will acquire more than half the enormous marine area that now passes under coastal state control.[6] At the same time, the provisions of the convention legalize absurdities. For instance, the Pitcairn Islands with 60 inhabitants may legally claim control over the resources of a maritime area several times larger than that which can be claimed by the Federal Republic of Germany with more than 60 million people. The Republic of Kiribati (the former Gilbert Islands) with about 55,000 inhabitants acquires rights over resources in a marine area larger than that which may be claimed by the People's Republic of China with more than one billion people.[7]

This is not to say that for many reasons some extension of coastal state jurisdiction in the marine environment may not be unavoidable, and the concept of a 200-nautical-mile exclusive economic zone conveniently consolidates into a single regime a variety of coastal state jurisdictional claims advanced over the past forty years.[8]

However, to be equitable the extension of coastal state control should be balanced, at least, by clear and definitive limits to national jurisdiction; by the development of an expanded concept of state responsibility, particularly with respect to resource management and protection of the marine environment; and by the establishment beyond national jurisdiction of a viable and meaningful international regime capable of filling the vacuum of the high seas and of compensating in some measure those countries that will suffer most from an extension of national jurisdiction in the oceans.

The convention lacks these balancing factors.

It does not clearly define the limits of national jurisdiction in ocean space nor, despite a number of general provisions,[9] does it seriously address the difficult problems of marine resource management. In fact most of the general provisions concerning management of marine resources are qualified or negated by subsequent specific provisions.[10]

Furthermore, the convention does not recognize that coastal states have any resource management responsibilities in their archipelagic waters, territorial sea, or legal continental shelf. A fundamental deficiency, finally, is the unstated assumption in the convention that all coastal states are both willing and able competently to manage marine living resources within their jurisdiction, an assumption that patently does not correspond to reality. Even if all coastal states did have this capacity, rational marine living resource management on a national basis would be impossible in the small marine areas allocated to the majority of coastal states.

No doubt even poor national management of marine living resources is preferable to freedom of fishing under contemporary conditions, but it is not the only alternative to freedom. There exists the concept that ocean space and its living and nonliving resources, beyond reasonable limits of national jurisdiction, are a common heritage of mankind and hence should be administered* by the international community for the benefit of all its members, both rich and poor.

The Flawed Rendering of the Common Heritage Principle

An international regime in ocean space beyond reasonable limits of national jurisdiction has become necessary, *inter alia,* for three purposes:

• It must fill the jurisdictional void that exists beyond national jurisdiction in order to prevent the total division of ocean space among coastal states.

---

*It is perhaps useful to clarify that, in the original concept, the common heritage of mankind was not *owned* by mankind (or by the international community, however defined) but *was held in trust* by mankind. Mankind through the international community had the *jus utendi* but not the *jus abutendi* or the right of disposal.

- It must ensure competent and nondiscriminatory resource management and conservation beyond national jurisdiction in order to prevent, insofar as possible, unnecessary destruction of resources.

- It must promote equity between states, while at the same time providing to all states benefits unobtainable under a national lake regime.

Very early in the recently concluded conference it became clear that the major maritime powers would tolerate a common heritage regime and related institutions only with respect to the seabed and its resources beyond national jurisdiction. Since the jurisdictional void of the high seas could not be filled, it became all the more important to create a universally useful common heritage regime and related institutions for the seabed. Unfortunately constructive objectives were largely forgotten in the almost theological debate that developed in Committee I of the conference. Compromise by the contending parties led to the drafting of a text that created a largely symbolic regime and excessively complicated institutions capable of efficiently carrying out few, if any, functions.

First, the convention does not attempt to define the limits of the seabed and ocean floor beyond the limits of national jurisdiction (the Area) supposedly administered by the future Authority. The Area is supposed to be defined indirectly as coastal states gradually establish the outer limits of their legal continental shelves under Article 76. It is a process expected to take at least ten years from the date of entry into force of the convention,[11] and the future Authority is totally excluded from influencing it in any way.[12] Thus the Authority could be faced with a situation in which it could not begin planning the exploitation of mineral resources because the nearest coastal states had not decided on the extent of their continental shelf claims.

Second, the scope of the common heritage regime and related institutions has been severely limited by defining the words "activities in the Area" to mean only activities of exploration for, and exploitation of, the mineral resources of the Area; by giving the word "resources"—which in the 1971 Declaration of Principles was understood to mean "living and nonliving resources"—the limited meaning of "mineral resources in situ," and by limiting the competence of the Authority in practice only to such resources (and not also to the Area as such), despite the explicit wording of Article 136 of the Convention;[13] by drafting a text that contemplates only the exploration and exploitation of manganese nodule deposits; and by defining in Article 76 the outer limits of the legal continental shelf in such a way as virtually to exclude the possibility of finding commercially exploitable hydrocarbon deposits in the Area. Thus the economic significance of the seabed area governed by the common heritage principle is much reduced.

Third, the development of manganese nodule deposits has been rendered unnecessarily complicated and expensive. The convention establishes unnecessary and unrealistic production controls in the international seabed area.[14] It creates a totally unnecessary "parallel system" of exploitation that is supposed to accommodate the interests of market economy countries, developing countries, and Socialist countries, but that in effect creates only an expensive bureaucratic system, the *initial* cost of which was estimated some years ago to range between $350 and $700 million.[15] It establishes a decision-making system for the Council of the future Authority that is almost certain to make timely and appropriate decisions impossible.[16]

These, among many other deficiencies, are likely to ensure that manganese nodule production in the Area will not be profitable for the foreseeable future. Thus, far from providing all states with benefits unobtainable under a national lake regime, it is likely that the common heritage system as implemented in the convention will prove to be an enduring economic burden on the international community. Indeed, there could be a danger that the future Authority's inability to administer seabed mineral resources effectively and efficiently might bring the principle of common heritage itself into disrepute and thus prejudice the future of equitable and cooperative development of resources in other areas beyond national jurisdiction, such as the moon and perhaps Antarctica.

Implementation of many provisions contained in the annexes to the convention relating to the seabed beyond national jurisdiction was indefinitely postponed by the adoption of Resolutions I and II at the 1982 Spring session of UNCLOS.[17] It might be possible for the Preparatory Commission of the Authority to use these resolutions to draft provisional rules, regulations, and procedures modifying some of the more unrealistic or burdensome provisions contained in, for instance, Annex III of the convention. Whether this will in fact be done will depend, of course, upon what action members of the Preparatory Commission decide to take.

Conclusion

Although the present convention reproduces, almost without change, most of the definitions and technical rules contained in the 1958 Geneva Conventions and adds a few more, it is to a far greater extent than these conventions a political document. As such the present convention is truly a "package deal" containing innumerable bilateral and multilateral political compromises. In fact, many of the legal rules established are sometimes based on nothing more substantial than political deals designed to accommodate the parochial interests of individual states.[18]

As a political document, the present convention reflects, although to a different extent and in different ways, both the predominant interests of politically predominant states and the general aspirations of the world community.

Thus from one point of view, the importance of the convention resides principally in the official recognition of the results of the ongoing enclosure movement in ocean space that benefits mainly the relatively few states possessing long coastlines fronting on the open seas. In this connection the convention is particularly deferential to a concept of state control in areas within coastal state jurisdiction, as wide and as unfettered as politically possible.*

It would not be right, however, to view the convention as reflecting only the perceived national interests of a relatively small group of states. Much of the rhetoric, several general provisions, and whole sections of the convention reflect—imperfectly, vaguely, sometimes even wrongheadedly—a general aspiration for a new order in the seas, based on international cooperation in

---

*Without prejudice, however, to navigational uses of the marine environment. These are safeguarded to some extent not only because the international community has a common interest in safeguarding freedom of trade but also because navigational uses of the sea closely affect the security interests of the major maritime powers.

meeting the needs of mankind as a whole. Unfortunately this new order remains essentially a rhetorical aspiration.

It is clear from what I have said that I consider the new convention on the law of the sea to be fatally flawed. Mankind has lost a truly historic opportunity to mold the legal framework governing activities in the marine environment in a way that contributes effectively to a just and equitable international order in the seas, responsive to the vital need for harmonization of marine uses and management of marine resources for the benefit of all.

Nevertheless we cannot reject the convention out of hand if we believe that it is important to maintain some semblance of global law of the sea or if we support the introduction of the principle of the common heritage of mankind into international law. Judgment of the usefulness of the present convention must also depend upon general considerations of public policy and upon whether the convention appears satisfactorily to protect national interests.

I would like to conclude with a paragraph from a 1970 U.S. State Department bulletin:

The stark fact is that the law of the sea is inadequate to meet the needs of modern technology and the concerns of the international community. If it is not modernized multilaterally, unilateral action and international conflict are inevitable. . . . The United States has a special responsibility to move this effort forward.[19]

These words are as true now as they were thirteen years ago. The present convention is not the end but rather the beginning of a long process that must eventually lead to a more rational and efficient use of our environment and a more equitable world order.

3

LEIGH S. RATINER

The Costs of American Rigidity

On 30 April 1982, the United States was the only Western industrialized country to vote against the final treaty adopted in
New York by the Third United Nations Conference on the Law of
the Sea. Venezuela, Turkey, and Israel also voted no. The USSR
and most Soviet bloc countries abstained, as did a few highly industrialized Western nations. Most of the West, including France
and Japan, joined the Third World and voted yes. Altogether, 130
nations voted to adopt the treaty and open it for signature.

The final treaty produced by the Third United Nations Conference on the Law of the Sea falls short of the goals sought by the
Reagan administration. It establishes a mixed economic system

Adapted from the author's "The Law of the Sea: A Crossroads for American Foreign Policy,"
Foreign Affairs 60 (Summer 1982): 1006–21. Some paragraphs have been deleted and the footnotes renumbered. Copyright © 1982, Council on Foreign Relations, Inc. Used by permission.

for the regulation and production of deep seabed minerals and the Reagan administration could not, as a matter of principle consistent with its free-enterprise philosophy, have done otherwise when the time came to vote.

Unfortunately, our strong and uncompromising defense of principle may have cost us a golden opportunity to convert the treaty into a better vehicle for commercial operators.

That loss could be minor, however, when compared with the prospect that the United States might now decide to exclude itself from a new global regulatory organization that may—probably sooner rather than later—count among its members all of our allies, the Third World, and the Socialist bloc. This new institution will safeguard the mining claims of our industrial competitors and reject rights claimed by American-flag companies.

Moreover, if the United States stays out of the sea law treaty while most major nations join it, we risk conflict over American assertions that we are entitled, without participating in the treaty, to rights embodied in it related to navigational freedoms, exclusive economic zones, jurisdiction over our continental shelf, fisheries, pollution control, and the conduct of marine scientific research.

Should all this come to pass (and it seems likely that it will) we will suffer a significant, long-term foreign policy setback with grave implications for U.S. influence in global economic and political affairs.

Divisions within the Reagan Administration

The Law of the Sea Treaty has been under negotiation since 1966, when the United States and the USSR agreed to consult all nations on the question of whether they would agree to a new global conference on the law of the sea. As initially envisaged, the aim of the conference was to fix the limit of the territorial sea at 12 miles and to provide for freedom of navigation through and over international straits overlapped by the new 12-mile limit.

In 1968 the United Nations began to expand the as-yet unwritten agenda of the conference to include the issue of deep seabed mining in areas beyond national jurisdiction. By the time the Law of the Sea Conference was formally created in 1973, its agenda included essentially all uses of the oceans. Between 1973 and 1980, over 150 countries, including the United States, agreed on treaty texts on all but four points: boundary delimitation, which was settled in the summer of 1981; participation in the treaty by entities that are not sovereign states; the composition and functions of the Preparatory Commission to set up the International Seabed Authority; and provisions for the protection of investment in deep seabed mining activities prior to entry into force of the treaty. After ten sessions of the conference and fourteen years of negotiating efforts, the new administration in Washington sought in the final conference session in spring 1982 to renegotiate essential elements of a package that already commanded widespread support and near consensus.

How did this come about? In March 1981, the new Reagan administration began a much-needed, soul-searching review of the draft convention on the law of the sea. It was clear that notwithstanding the treaty's many potential benefits, its deep seabed mining provisions were anathema to some elements of the Reagan administration; moreover, the treaty was considered unratifiable in the Senate. The U.S. policy review lasted more than a year.

The policy review was—as are many conducted through interagency groups regardless of the administration in power—essentially an adversarial process in which initially all documents were prepared for the purpose of reaching preconceived objectives and prejudicing an ultimate decision. Pressure from the White House to reach consensus was intense, and this produced even further (and in some cases, devastating) compromise formulations describing fundamental issues in dispute.

There were two general points of view that emerged in the review process. The first was advocated by the deputy assistant secretary of state for ocean and fisheries affairs, the most senior official responsible for the day-to-day conduct of the review. In essence, this point of view held that the treaty was flawed because it created adverse precedents for other negotiations on economic issues between developed and developing nations (the North-South dialogue); subjugated American industry to an international regulatory and management system; and was incompatible with President Reagan's apparent desire to return the United States to a period of power and influence in world affairs in which its policies would simply be enunciated rather than sold to others through a process of diplomacy and negotiation. I think it is also fair to say that proponents of this view did not believe that it was possible for any American to participate actively in the negotiation of the treaty without being seduced by it; they therefore saw great risks in any return to the bargaining table, even for the purpose of making a best effort. These views were strongly supported by staff on the domestic side of the White House, by the Department of Interior, and by some civilians in the defense establishment, as well as some members of Congress.

The opposite point of view was represented by other agencies and participants in the process and by this author, who at the time was serving as a contract advisor to Assistant Secretary of State James L. Malone. That position can best be summarized as a recognition that the treaty in its present form was unratifiable, accompanied by a belief that it could be renegotiated and significant improvements made to it. From the perspective of those who held this point of view, there seemed no harm in trying to improve the treaty in fundamental ways because, in the long run, a good treaty that provided universal recognition of mining claims as well as universal acceptance of countless other important legal principles would be a worthwhile goal. Moreover, the proponents of this viewpoint felt that U.S. interests could not be compromised merely by a return to the negotiations, since the president ultimately would have to decide whether the United States should sign the treaty.

Another point made with respect to resuming negotiations: responsible American negotiators, acting under strict instructions, would not be lured into accepting a treaty that was contrary to the overall national interest. American negotiators at a multilateral conference generally do not operate in a vacuum or in secret. All of their tactical and strategic movements are discussed and debated on a daily basis with the wide array of U.S. interests represented in the U.S. delegation.[1] Opportunities for the loyal opposition to change the direction of the negotiations are legion. Therefore, the perceived risk by some of compromising national interests through an effort to renegotiate did not seem sufficiently realistic to sacrifice the opportunity to improve the treaty.

This view prevailed, and the president decided on 29 January 1982 that the United States would return to the negotiations and

seek six broad objectives. These objectives were then supplemented by detailed instructions, which were not sent to the president for approval but were negotiated among the various agencies
that had participated in the initial process. Perhaps inevitably,
the development of detailed instructions became a surrogate
forum for returning to the original issue that had already been
decided by the president. The basic dispute over the instructions
was whether to make them so strict and confining as to produce a
situation in which it would be impossible for American negotiators
to satisfy them.

When finally issued on 8 March, long after the preliminary
negotiations in New York had begun, the instructions reflected an
interpretation of the president's objectives that was considerably
more constrained than the objectives themselves. It is for this
reason that many delegations at the conference frequently found
it difficult to understand the U.S. negotiating posture, since the
president's public statement appeared to a reasonable reader to
permit a far more flexible U.S. stance than was actually being presented. Other delegations did not understand that the U.S. delegation was operating under instructions containing a restrictive interpretation of the president's objectives and was under pressure
to adhere to them as the sole guidance for interpretation.

One final point in the policy review process turned out to be of
utmost importance in the end. Since one of the principal U.S. objectives was to secure access to the raw materials of the deep
seabed, the question necessarily arose as to whether there was
any alternative to a comprehensive treaty on the law of the sea
that would adequately protect claimed mining rights and thus provide a stable basis for major financial commitments in support of
deep seabed mining. The proponents of withdrawal from the conference argued forcefully that an alternative mini-treaty regime
among the genuinely concerned industrialized countries—outside
the framework of the comprehensive treaty—would be an adequate basis for investment even if a treaty on the law of the sea
were adopted by a very large number of countries and entered into
force. Those who favored returning to the bargaining table were
divided on this issue. Some felt that under certain conditions a viable alternative mini-treaty regime could be established, but that
the United States should nevertheless seek the comprehensive

treaty solution. Others felt that an alternative mini-treaty regime would be resisted by our Western allies in the face of a treaty adopted by the vast majority of nations, including virtually all of the developing countries. Moreover, it was felt that if a comprehensive treaty on the law of the sea entered into force for 100 nations or more, mining companies would eventually choose that regime—which would give the best color of title to their mining claims—rather than a separate mini-treaty regime.

Because views were divided among those who supported returning to the bargaining table, doubts about the realistic prospects for establishing an alternative mini-treaty were not forcefully put forward at the highest levels of government, although the issue appeared in the relevant documents as one on which there was disagreement. Related arguments were presented to support particular points of view. As a result, to the best of my knowledge the president and his close advisors received no authoritative statement that, if they wished to preserve direct access to strategic raw materials through American-flag operations, there could be no viable alternative to an improved comprehensive treaty on the law of the sea.

Accordingly, when a final decision was made and detailed instructions for the delegation were negotiated, there was an assumption in the administration that if the United States adopted a tough uncompromising stance and lost the opportunity to improve the treaty as a result, it could afford to stay out of the treaty because there was a viable alternative—a separate mini-treaty with our allies. This assumption may have been the Achilles heel of U.S. strategy for the last session of the Law of the Sea Conference. (Moreover, the strong U.S. public posture to push ahead with mini-treaty negotiations even before the Law of the Sea Conference began in March was a major factor in convincing the developing countries that the United States did not have a serious interest in the comprehensive treaty, and thus worsened the chances for successfully negotiating the president's objectives.)

One further comment should be made in connection with the policy review process. The Defense Department in previous administrations had been a strong unyielding supporter of the successful conclusion of the treaty. It had always felt that the stability of international law that would accrue from this treaty, which contains many provisions favorable to the mobility of our air and sea forces, was a significant benefit to national security when compared with the uncertainty of potential arguments with coastal states that might occur in the absence of the treaty.

During the Reagan administration, however, two things changed in the Defense Department's stance. First, much greater emphasis was placed, particularly in the civilian side of the department, on the importance of American access to strategic raw materials as a national security interest. Second, there was a belief that if the treaty finally entered into force without U.S. participation, most of the provisions favorable to the security of the United States would be accepted as customary international law, and that treaty rights would therefore be available to all states whether or not they became parties to the treaty. In combination, these two views produced significantly less enthusiasm for the treaty within the Defense Department than had been the case before. This shift markedly changed the balance of power in the intragovernmental adversarial process. The assumption that the treaty provisions would become customary international law was never seriously questioned—it was taken for granted.

The American Ideological Straitjacket

Out of respect for our power and influence, the world waited for the U.S. decision. The Law of the Sea Conference went into neutral gear, avoiding final adoption of the text that had been virtually completed in 1980 with apparent U.S. agreement. By the time President Reagan announced on 29 January that the United States would return to the negotiating table, U.S. negotiating leverage was substantial.

When the conference resumed in March, the United States had its golden opportunity. The rest of the world was ready, willing, and anxious to reshape important aspects of the treaty to attract U.S. support. Yet in the end, the text was adopted over U.S. objections. The Soviet bloc abstention was prompted by a minor point, and they have now signed the treaty. Despite high-level pleas for solidarity, two of America's closest allies, Japan and France, voted in favor of the treaty—a startling and potentially powerful signal about Japanese postwar foreign policy development. West Ger-

many, Britain, and a handful of other Western allies abstained in
support of the United States—but may well sign the treaty with or
without us, for reasons that will be discussed later.

The United States returned to the bargaining table with instructions to fix every important defect in the seabed mining
provisions—in short, to convert the treaty into the "frontier mining code" in which the first company to stake a claim owns the
resources and is not subject to regulation or management except
for the payment of taxes. This view was combined with a demand
for overwhelming voting power for the United States and its
closest allies in the proposed International Seabed Authority.

All of the improvements we sought were desirable and important. Some of them were fundamental to making the treaty commercially more workable. But the primary U.S. objective, in fact,
was the eradication of ideological impurity. As a result, when the
time came for compromise, the United States did not make
ideological concessions to the Third World in exchange for pragmatic improvements. The Western allies maintained solidarity
with the United States throughout the negotiations; and because
in varying degrees our allies share our ideological views but not
our willingness to sacrifice concrete accomplishments for them,
they were deterred from negotiating more modest improvements
on their own behalf.

Our strong stance on every issue (combined with public postur-
ing in favor of an urgent separate mini-treaty) persuaded the bulk
of conference participants that the U.S. appetite was too great—
no improvements likely to satisfy us could also be swallowed by
the Third World. Many hoped until the final hours that the United
States would moderate its position on other issues, to create a
fruitful negotiating climate. Finally we did, but our concessions
were small when measured against our remaining demands. Indeed, even the few concessions we offered brought cries of sellout
from some in Congress, the mining industry, and elements of the
executive branch.

The U.S. delegation was therefore held in check and did not
make serious compromise proposals on many issues where gen-
uine compromise might have produced far-reaching improvements in the treaty text. For example, if the United States had not
demanded virtually autocratic ruling powers over the Seabed

Authority and had not sought total elimination of the so-called production ceiling, it would have been possible, perhaps easy, to have obtained major improvements in the practical effects of, and the principles contained in, the technology transfer provisions and the provisions that permit amendments to the treaty (after twenty years) without U.S. consent. When the U.S. position did reflect modest relaxation in some of these areas, the negotiators came very close to solutions to these latter two problems.

It should be borne in mind that those who did not want the United States to participate in the conference may also have had as their underlying tactical objective a desire to ensure that the treaty was not improved, so as to make it difficult for our Western allies to join the treaty and concomitantly to make it easier when the conference ended in failure to obtain rapid agreement to an alternative mini-treaty regime.

The developing countries, however, sensed that these dynamics might be in process and virtually demanded an opportunity to negotiate the one issue on which they were prepared to make a concession significant enough to lure our allies into the treaty. Paralyzed by the rigidity of its constructions, the American delegation had no choice but to play into the hands of the Third World and negotiate the issue that the developing countries insisted be taken up first: the recognition of rights for mining companies that had already made investments in the seabed.

This was because the issue of "grandfather rights" was considered by the entire conference to be "outstanding," for it had never been part of the 1980 package negotiated by American Ambassador Elliot Richardson. Moreover, it was an issue on which significant progress could be made, while issues the United States wished to renegotiate were among the most difficult. The developing countries hoped that if they made meaningful concessions on grandfather rights, the U.S. mining industry would be pacified and would reduce its pressure on the U.S. government. In turn, they assumed the United States would reduce its demands.

Negotiations on the issue of grandfather rights resulted in a final conference resolution that successfully met some of our fundamental objectives—and, more important, may well have met the most central objective held by our closest allies. Under the resolution, four existing mining consortia (each of which includes or is controlled by U.S. companies) plus projects sponsored by the governments of Japan, France, the USSR, and India would have guaranteed automatic access to the strategic raw materials of the seabed for the first generation of seabed mining. Altogether, ten seabed mining entities were entitled to all of the mineral production likely or possible from the seabed for the next thirty to fifty years; metal market projections indicate that demand for manganese, copper, cobalt, and nickel from the seabed is unlikely to reach, much less exceed, the production capacity of these grand-fathered miners during that period.

Thus, with the notable exceptions of mandatory technology transfer and the procedure for amending the treaty, the offensive ideological provisions of the treaty would not effectively apply before the middle of the twenty-first century. By that time there would have been a thorough treaty review and an opportunity to renegotiate.

Because the issue of grandfather rights dominated the negotiations, and because the negotiations were up against a deadline of 30 April (a consensus decision accepted by the Reagan administration in 1981), opportunities to deal with issues other than grandfather rights did not arise until the final ten days of the session. Moreover, the procedure for the final session of the conference was organized in such a way that between 13 April and 30 April the only amendments to the treaty that would have any chance of inclusion in the final draft would be those put forward by the president of the conference, Ambassador Tommy T. B. Koh of Singapore, if he were satisfied that such amendments adequately enhanced the prospects for consensus.

For a little over two weeks the president of the conference held enormous power over the final treaty text. At the same time, it was his responsibility—and to his credit he took it seriously—to introduce amendments to the treaty only if they enhanced the prospects for consensus. He organized small groups for rapid, effective negotiations on other issues.

However, the atmosphere in this final stage was undoubtedly affected by an important exchange earlier in the conference. Ambassador Koh had hoped that a set of proposed amendments put forward very early in the negotiations by a group of so-called "Good Samaritans"* would bridge the gap between the developing countries, on the one hand, and the United States and its Western allies on the other. He wanted both sides to accept these propositions—or at least not reject them—so that at the end of the conference he would be in a position to propose them for incorporation into the final treaty text. For the United States, these papers moved significantly toward meeting the president's publicly announced objectives, although they fell far short of the American delegation's negotiating instructions. Verbatim acceptance of the Good Samaritan papers would have produced a treaty that on a fair reading of the president's objectives of 29 January would still have fallen short.

The crucial question was whether the United States was willing to send a strong signal that these papers were by and large on the right track, and that further negotiations and additional amendments might make them acceptable. While the United States did not intend to reject these proposals out of hand, it stated its difficulties with them in such strong terms as to lead conference leaders to conclude that they had been rejected. In the vocabulary of diplomats, strong reservations to a proposal are generally considered to be a rejection. Thus, at the crucial halfway point in the conference there may have been a tragic failure of communication.

After the United States apparently rejected the Good Samaritan papers as a basis for negotiations, the remaining weeks of negotiation were carried out by the president of the conference in a desultory and pessimistic atmosphere, even though time permitted serious negotiation of the main issues of concern to the United States. Although the Group of 77 was maintaining a very tough posture in response to the U.S. stance, the job could have been done. But in an atmosphere where hope and optimism were lacking and U.S. commitment to the negotiation was doubted, it became virtually impossible for the president to pull the rabbit out of the hat.

Koh did, nevertheless, finally make a number of additional improvements to the treaty as a result of direct negotiations between the Western countries and the developing countries. For example,

---

*Canada, Australia, New Zealand, Norway, Sweden, Denmark, Finland, Iceland, the Netherlands, and Ireland.

the United States is guaranteed a seat on the executive council of the new global institution, the Seabed Authority (assuming, of course, that the United States joins the treaty). The mechanisms for amending the seabed mining provisions of the treaty have been improved. The contract approval system for mining entities has less potential for abuse and discretion. The policy orientation of the Seabed Authority is slightly more favorable to mineral production, and the Authority must adopt rules and regulations for newly discovered seabed minerals once a nation capable of exploiting them makes a request—thus avoiding one of the fatal flaws in the previous draft treaty, a moratorium on these other minerals.

These achievements were modest, however, and did not rectify fundamental inequities and adverse precedents that the administration quite properly opposed. Nevertheless, they may be sufficient to make the treaty very attractive to other Western industrialized countries that, while sharing our ideological views, are more interested in assured access to strategic raw materials and influence in global economic decision-making. Under the treaty, they will be guaranteed mineral access for a substantial period into the future and will play a large role in shaping the rules for seabed mining.

Limits of the Mini-Treaty Option

Perhaps the greatest irony for the United States is that, as a result of one further change in the last stages of the conference, the treaty now authorizes—even commands—what the Third World had long vehemently opposed: a mini-treaty among those countries that wish immediately to resolve overlapping minesite claims and obtain global approval for their legal rights. But there is a catch. To obtain global approval they must sign the treaty.

If the nations fail to sign, and instead sign an *alternative* mini-treaty regime, they will provoke global disapproval of the lawfulness of their mining claims. The president of the conference has vowed to challenge any alternative mini-treaty before the UN General Assembly and to seek an opinion from the International Court of Justice. The resulting protracted litigation would have a chilling effect on seabed mineral investment.

For this and other reasons, West Germany, Britain, and most

other potential seabed mining nations ultimately will sign the Law of the Sea Treaty and a mini-treaty *among themselves* that will dovetail with the comprehensive treaty. In any event, our allies will surely make certain that any such mini-treaty preserves their option to sign the Law of the Sea Treaty. They will do so because the Law of the Sea Treaty creates unchallengeable rights, superior to those created by a mini-treaty. Lacking enough ability to persuade its allies to sign a permanent mini-treaty as an alternative to the LOS Treaty, the United States ultimately will be abandoned by those allies, who will be prohibited from recognizing U.S. mini-treaty site claims once they sign the treaty.[2]

This point is crucial, because I believe the U.S. decision not to compromise ideological issues was founded on an assumption that after the conference ended, the Western industrialized countries would ignore the Law of the Sea Treaty and set up an alternate mini-treaty. This approach presumably assumed that a mini-treaty would include all potential seabed mining countries and therefore would provide sufficient legal security to attract the billions of dollars of private capital necessary to set up commercial mining operations. I suspect that if William Safire had understood that this outcome was, at best, improbable and unworkable, he would not have suggested in *The New York Times* on 9 April 1982 that the United States shelve the treaty negotiations. I believe that if President Reagan understood the realistic prospects for an alternative mini-treaty regime, he too would have had second thoughts about the pursuit of principle over pragmatism.

U.S. policymakers may have also made another assumption that could prove dangerously false: that the United States could stay outside the treaty but claim and enjoy its numerous beneficial provisions (which, among other things, establish rights to the 200-mile economic zone, guarantee to every coastal state broad jurisdiction over its continental shelf, and provide for freedom of, through, and over international straits),[3] and that these claimed benefits would be accepted by other nations because the treaty reflects custom, an accepted way of formulating international law.

I do not believe that serious consideration was given to the possibility that the contrary argument could be made—that the Law of the Sea Treaty creates rights only for those who are parties to it and who assume the treaty's obligations. Let us look at a few

examples. The Strait of Gibraltar is critical to the passage of surface and submerged vessels and to overflight by U.S. aircraft.
Spain, which is the relevant coastal sovereign, might argue that
the 12-mile territorial sea has become part of customary law (a
view very widely held in the world community). At the same time,
Spain might argue that the regime of enlarged "transit passage"
through international straits is new to international law, that it is
found only in the Law of the Sea Treaty and is thus a contract
among the parties in it. Thus Spain would argue that the old rule
permitting only "innocent passage" in the territorial sea would apply—which prohibits submerged navigation. This is not the time
or place to attempt to prejudge the outcome of such an argument.
What is dangerous for the United States is the existence of the
argument and the potential uncertainty of U.S. military rights in
narrow seas during times of crisis.

In a second example, coastal states could choose to impose
stricter regulations on oil tankers flying a U.S. flag, arguing that
they have a right to discriminate against nonparties to the treaty.
Third, in a Middle East crisis Arab countries might be tempted to
seize on U.S. nonparticipation in the treaty as an excuse to attempt to limit our activities within their economic zones.

Thus, while treaty rights may be claimed as a matter of customary law, they may also be contested (even by obstructive action)
and in any case challenged in protracted litigation before the International Court of Justice. That court may one day resolve
America's rights to freedom of navigation, leaving open the
possibility that the successful ten-year negotiating effort to gain
these rights could conceivably be lost in a single court decision.

Possible Loss of American Influence

One final point remains. The totality of the seabed mining provisions of the treaty is hard to defend on the merits. I am a conservative who sympathizes with the Reagan administration's criticisms
of the Law of the Sea Treaty; presumably that is why the Reagan
administration asked me to join the effort at renegotiation. And
while I am certain that the final treaty would have better satisfied
U.S. interests had the administration been less ideologically rigid
in its approach, I also would be the first to acknowledge that the

best that could have been done would have involved important compromises of principle.

But the dilemma for the United States now goes far beyond the specific flaws in this treaty. In time—probably sooner rather than later—our allies, the Soviet bloc, and the Third World will sign and ratify the treaty. They see a long-term future in the treaty, and they will want to be part of it. They will want to protect grandfather rights for their companies, secure international approval for broad jurisdiction over their continental shelves, have a voice in organizing, staffing, and drafting the rules of the new Seabed Authority, and lay to rest numerous other potential disputes about varying uses of ocean space and resources.

If the Western industrialized powers, minus the United States, join the Soviet bloc and the Third World, they will create a historic global organization—one that for the first time regulates, manages, and produces globally shared resources. One day this institution could use its taxing power to become self-financing. Should all this occur without American influence, participation, or leadership, our nation will suffer a much more serious adverse precedent than any of the adverse precedents we fought against in the treaty negotiation itself. We will stand as the emperor without clothes—for the entire world will see that it can do amazing and stupendous things without American money, leadership, or technology. If the United States is not part of the treaty system, American companies will have to go to other countries to be able to conduct business in the seabed. As a result, the United States will lose direct access to strategic raw materials from the seabed, a goal it has sought consistently throughout the ten-year law of the sea negotiations.

In short, the guardians of pure conservative ideology may have won a battle when the United States stood alone at the Law of the Sea Conference, but we may lose a very important war. If my political analysis is correct, this or some future administration will come to understand that the costs of isolation are far higher than the costs of accepting some of the rhetoric and principles of the North-South dialogue. And when the United States does eventually join, the rules of the game will already be set and our industrial competitors will be operating in the seabed and will have gained by then major political and economic advantages in the work of the new institution.

Our senior foreign policy makers should understand that once leadership is abdicated and the world finds it can proceed without us, it will not be easy for the United States to reclaim its influence.

4

W. SCOTT BURKE

FRANK S. BROKAW

Ideology and the Law
of the Sea

The United States should not sign the Treaty on the Law of the Sea (LOS). It seriously conflicts with American interests and is radically opposed to the long-term political and economic strength of the West. The treaty's immediate disadvantages concern the terms governing deep seabed mining, but potentially far more grave are the precedents the treaty may establish in other economic and political areas. The seabed mining provisions of the convention spring from an ideology that favors supranational control of the world's resources and wholesale redistribution of wealth and power. If the United States were to sign this treaty, it would accept in principle standards of international law and economic justice that would undoubtedly be extended to other important areas. Once these standards are accepted in one context,

The opinions presented in this chapter are the authors' own and do not necessarily reflect the positions of the United States Department of State or Security Pacific National Bank.

it will be difficult to rationalize resistance to their application in another.

Underdeveloped states and various organs of the United Nations for years have advanced theories to justify massive resource transfers from the West to the Third World and to international organizations. In the Law of the Sea Treaty, they have established a mechanism for achieving this goal through its central principle that the deep seabed resources are the "common heritage of mankind." If the scheme established by the convention succeeds, the West will face rising demands for acceptance of the same principles in existing multilateral institutions, such as the International Monetary Fund (IMF) and the World Bank, and in new areas where no legal norms or institutions have been established firmly, such as Antarctica's resources, radio and television frequencies, the allocation of telecommunication satellite orbits, and rules governing extraterrestrial bodies.

The Law of the Sea Treaty represents the first formal codification and implementation of the essential ideas underlying the New International Economic Order (NIEO), which calls for large-scale redistributions from the developed world to the Third World. As such, the treaty ratifies, in effect, a disquieting trend in the behavior of the World Bank, as well as Western private and central banks. That the precepts of the NIEO are already influencing major Western financial institutions is disturbing. But formal codification of these principles in the treaty marks a major change, laying the groundwork for extension into other policy arenas. Such a fundamental shift in international economic relationships would have unfortunate effects on both the developed and developing worlds.

Background

To understand the full implications of the Law of the Sea Treaty, one must understand it as part of a series of demands made by the Third World, or the Group of 77 (as it has come to be called), on the developed countries. In broadest terms, these demands form the basis of the NIEO, first announced in 1974 in a United Nations General Assembly declaration[1] and supported by two other resolutions: the Charter of Economic Rights and Duties of States (the Economic Charter) and the Declaration of Principles.

The NIEO and the Economic Charter that gives it shape are a moral challenge. They set forth a plan for the comprehensive alteration of the world economic system. The moral claim is that disparities in income between states are unjust and are caused by unfair economic arrangements, the lingering effects of colonialism, and the depredations of multinational corporations. NIEO supporters not only deplore income disparities between states but also condemn the standard of living in the West as an excessive consumption of scarce resources by the fortuitously privileged. They claim that bilateral foreign aid is restrictive and inadequate, that Western dominance of technology perpetuates their inferior status, and that existing international economic institutions are rigged to force them to remain sources of raw material.

This broad analysis has provided the basis of evolving Third World claims against the developed countries. After the emergence of Africa and Asia from colonial rule, these claims began with arguments that large wealth transfers from the West to the Third World were justified on rationales of either charity (the rich should help the poor) or guilt (the former colonial powers should atone for racism and domination). These arguments were supplemented by some Western observers, who appealed more recently to self-interest: that the wealthier countries should encourage the economic growth of developing nations to increase markets for Western exports, and that relieving poverty in the Third World will forestall conflicts that could affect the West.

Despite escalating assistance and loans from the West, Third World spokesmen and borrowers remain dissatisfied. Direct aid from national governments has strings attached and loans must in theory be repaid. President Julius Nyerere of Tanzania gave voice to widespread Third World feelings on this issue:

I am saying, it is not right that the vast majority of the world's population should be forced into the position of beggars, without dignity. In one world, as in one state, when I am rich because you are poor, and I am poor because you are rich, the transfer of wealth from rich to poor is a matter of right; it is not an appropriate matter for charity. The objective must be the eradication of poverty and the establishment of a minimum standard of living for all people. This will involve its converse—a ceiling on wealth for individuals and nations, as well as deliberate action to transfer resources from the rich to the poor within and across national boundaries.[2]

Paradoxically, the massive transfer of resources demanded by Nyerere and others has already occurred. As will be discussed below, it has been carried out by private banks in the West on a scale beyond the demands of envy and resentment. But grants can be demeaning and loans are not dependable. A Western government might change the terms of its assistance or reduce or eliminate certain programs. The United States, for instance, stopped military assistance to Chile, Guatemala, and Argentina because of human rights concerns and withdrew economic aid to Cuba and Nicaragua for assisting forces opposed to friendly governments. This is anything but an ideal state of affairs for aid recipients.

The NIEO and the Response of Western Financial Institutions

In the broad climate produced by these mounting demands on the developed nations, a series of fundamental changes has begun to occur in Western political and economic institutions. Until now, the changes have been significant, but still—to this point—informal. The most obvious of these has occurred in the behavior of Western financial institutions.

In the past half-dozen years, transfers of funds to the Third World in the form of cash grants and loans have increased very rapidly from international lending institutions such as the World Bank and the regional multilateral banks. At the same time, private Western banks vastly increased syndicated loans to private and sovereign borrowers in the less-developed countries (LDCs). Approximately $640 billion in loans are outstanding today to non-oil-producing LDCs, compared to $200 billion six years ago.[3] Many of these loans were directly guaranteed by Western governments. Recent recommendations that the World Bank's lending authority be increased and that the U.S. Treasury and the IMF intervene to ensure the successful rescheduling of Latin American debt may cause substantial erosion of the standards these institutions have used to screen requests for assistance in the past. Continued rescheduling of existing debt and originations of new loans will increase still further the resources available to the Third World. Serious questions have arisen whether the loans currently outstanding can be repaid; and if they are not, they must ultimately be written off or be assumed by Western central banks.[4]

As we noted, this evolving pattern of behavior and policy from international lending institutions represents only an informal acquiescence in the ideas underlying the NIEO. But this background brings us to consideration of the first formal codification of these principles in the Law of the Sea Treaty, in a framework explicitly built on a claim of right.

The Law of the Sea Treaty

The Group of 77 (G–77) ultimately seeks a means to compel transfers of wealth from the West, in effect by taxing individuals and institutions in the developed countries. Such a system would eliminate most of the undesirable features of bilateral assistance and borrowing. It would reduce the influence of donor countries and the multilateral banks while simultaneously increasing the flexibility and power of recipients. Because developed countries would not consent to such direct taxation, however, the Group of 77 had to find less overtly threatening means to tap the West's wealth. The Law of the Sea Treaty negotiations furnished that opportunity.

The seabed mining provisions of the Law of the Sea Treaty reflect the values and institutional arrangements favored by the NIEO. Spokesmen for the developing nations have been candid about their intentions. The mining regime "should be a democratic institution responsible for bridging the gap between the rich countries and the poor countries and establishing a fairer and more just system of international relations."[5] The treaty supports the goals of the NIEO by creating a supranational "Authority" with taxing and licensing powers and the right to mandate technology transfer and to establish and operate a mining entity (the "Enterprise") subsidized by and competing with its "licensees."

The Negotiations

Only a few developed nations possess the capital, technology, and human resources sufficient to exploit the deep seabed. The developing states lack any such capacity. Barring some major extrinsic Third World bargaining counter, therefore, one might expect that the developed nations could have dominated negotiations on the law applied to this activity. Yet they did not. And in fact it was the U.S. that proposed the parallel seabed mining system under the treaty. This failure by the developed nations is explained in part by the power of ideas to shape events.

A Third World representative to the UN set the tone for the UNCLOS negotiations in a speech to the United Nations in 1967. He declared that the deep seabed was beyond national jurisdiction and that its resources were the "common heritage of mankind." He left this term undefined. Although both the industrial and the developing nations accepted this concept in principle, they could not agree on its meaning. The industrial states for a time argued that the seabed belonged to no one and was thus subject to development by anyone *(res nullius)*. Third World spokesmen asserted that it belonged to everyone to be exploited for and enjoyed by all *(res communis)*.[6] The *res nullius* interpretation would permit those capable of mining the seabed to do so and retain whatever benefits resulted.

The G−77 advanced a novel variant[7] of the *res communis* construction that would permit them to control and appropriate the benefits of exploitation of the ocean floor despite their inability to contribute anything to seabed development. These states asserted unilaterally that the common heritage principle could be interpreted only within the context of the NIEO as defined by the Economic Charter and the Declaration of Principles. They argued that these resolutions of the General Assembly had supplanted custom as declaratory of international law as applied to deep sea mining. Confusion over the correct definition of the common heritage principle provided the context in which the Third World has attempted to shape the mining regime along the lines of the NIEO.

The *res nullius* construction, which is consistent with traditional high seas freedoms and with their domestic institutions, was in the interests of the developed countries. But instead of pushing vigorously for it, when the negotiations deadlocked Western representatives apparently became persuaded that the definition of common heritage was really only an ideological abstraction and therefore of little consequence. More concerned about freedom of navigation because of its immediate military importance than about rules to be applied to an uncertain and as yet nonexistent business activity, the U.S. negotiators at UNCLOS acquiesced to the Third World's *res communis* construction. Accordingly, the G—77's concept of the rights over the seabed determined the boundaries of the debate and ensured that whatever seabed mining regime emerged from UNCLOS would reflect a variant of *res communis* rather than the version favorable to the West. The acceptance of what then appeared a benign or at least unthreatening concept was to have harsh consequences, in part because of another major concession made by the West—that all issues surrounding the law of the sea were to be negotiated in one grand forum.

Addressing so many difficult issues in the same negotiations ensured that the proceedings would be mired in complexity and that concessions in one area would be traded for benefits in another. Moreover, because all states were entitled to participate, patterns prevalent in other multilateral fora appeared in UNCLOS. Anti-Western rhetoric and Third World demands for resource transfers became important elements in the proceedings. Because most participants had few if any tangible interests in the law of the sea, they could advance ambitious ideological demands on nations that had an important stake in the substantive outcome. Because Third World agreement was required for the convention to become effective, Western negotiators were strongly influenced to make concessions to states whose only negotiating asset was the formal right to assent to or reject the treaty.

Once these two concessions had been made, a treaty with undesirable provisions was a foregone conclusion. Able lawyers and professional diplomats were assigned by successive American administrations to negotiate the best deal possible.[8] These representatives focused upon the immediate problem of obtaining practical, short-term benefits for their country. Insofar as deep seabed mining was concerned, the crucial issue of principle had already been conceded. Thus their role was to minimize the damage to American interests in the mining provisions and to trade agreement to the mining scheme for benefits in other areas, principally the right to travel through strategically important straits. Unfortunately, however, it is not clear that the treaty confers significant advantages on the United States.[9]

Ideology and "Pragmatism"

Advocates of the treaty take different positions on the ideological features of the convention. Most American supporters express mild disapproval of the ideology underlying the deep seabed mining provisions but dismiss them as relatively insignificant.[10] Others ignore the offending features altogether, focusing on short-term gains they allege may accrue to the United States under the treaty.[11] Some treaty supporters simply dismiss opposition as ideological and therefore of little weight.[12]

Unfortunately, the ideology of the treaty cannot be ignored. It gave birth to the seabed mining provisions; it determined the institutions the treaty creates; and it established precedents that may govern negotiations in other policy arenas. The treaty is an ideological document. Third World advocates of the treaty and their Western sympathizers are well aware of the significance of the convention's ideology and cite it as its greatest strength.

Leigh S. Ratiner's arguments in favor of the treaty, published elsewhere in this book, illustrate some of these patterns. Ratiner concedes that "the totality of the seabed mining provisions is hard to defend on the merits," yet he criticizes the Reagan administration for opposing the convention. He argues that a strong defense of principle may cost the United States the opportunity to convert the treaty into a better vehicle for commercial operations, and asserts that if "grandfather rights" were guaranteed to Western companies the offensive ideological features of the treaty would not apply until the middle of the twenty-first century. He criticizes the Reagan administration for its unwillingness to "make ideological concessions to the Third World in exchange for pragmatic improvements." Ratiner claims that some future American president will sign the treaty, and that the document signed will be worse than if we had compromised earlier on principle so as to gain additional benefits. In sum, Ratiner rejects the significance of the treaty's ideological flaws and advocates "pragmatic" concession of principle in return for concrete benefits.

Ratiner asserts that American failure to ratify the treaty and negotiation of an alternative treaty with like-minded Western nations may lead the Group of 77 to challenge the contending regime in the UN General Assembly and seek a disapproving opinion of the International Court of Justice (ICJ). He also claims that if the Seabed Authority created by the convention flourishes without American participation, a precedent may be set as the world learns it can do great things without the United States.

Arguments in favor of the UNCLOS convention, including Ratiner's, often focus more on what are feared will be the negative consequences of rejection than on the expectation of benefits. One such fear is that Third World states will challenge any mini-treaty in the General Assembly and the World Court. No doubt the General Assembly will not make deep seabed exploitation an exception to its long-standing practice of endorsing institutions and policies harmful to Western interests. But disapproval of the General Assembly can have no practical effect if cosigners are determined to proceed with implementation of an alternative treaty.

A challenge in the ICJ to the alternative mini-treaty may occur. Decisions of the court, which are advisory, are extremely difficult to predict and depend on the court's composition at the time. In any event, it is unlikely that the court would declare noncompliance with UNCLOS illegal, especially in the face of a ratified and functioning alternative treaty.

As a practical matter, of course, the court has no power to compel nonsignatories to adhere to UNCLOS, even if it should declare their legal obligation to do so. An adverse court opinion would carry some political weight, it is true, but it is doubtful that such weight would exceed the political cost the Western powers already would have borne by refusing to sign the treaty in the first instance. On the other hand, at a time when the Western states are an increasingly beleaguered minority in the UN, it seems absurd to claim that failure to acquiesce in the majority will entail any special disadvantages for either the United States or the West in general.

Ratiner's assertion that grandfather rights for "pioneer" miners mitigate the treaty's offensive elements by postponing their entry into force until the twenty-first century is not reassuring. The next century will begin in seventeen years. Although seabed mining probably will not be economically feasible for several decades, the assimilation into customary international law of principles harmful to the economic well-being of the West would proceed with accelerating momentum.

Ratiner fears that a successful Seabed Authority will set an unfortunate precedent because the world will learn that it can attain important ends without the United States. It is doubtful that the treaty's regime can succeed without participation of the United States and other major industrial nations. T. Vincent Learson, the Ford administration representative to UNCLOS, states, "They have nothing unless we are in it."[13] If the United States succeeds in persuading most of the small number of Western nations capable of seabed mining to join it in an alternative treaty, the UNCLOS convention will be ineffectual. There is a strong chance that the United States may accomplish this objective.[14]

The magnitude of the capital investment and operating costs required to mine the seabed greatly limits the countries and firms that can undertake the activity. The barriers to production and the tax burden created by the treaty make it questionable whether any mining companies can operate under the UNCLOS convention without massive subsidies and guarantees from their national governments.[15] Northcutt Ely, counsel to Ocean Mining Associates, asserts that no unsubsidized company could adhere to its terms, and that American companies "would not be able to finance or conduct operations under the terms of the proposed treaty."[16] He states, "(T)he treaty gives the investor neither the assurance of access to seabed minerals nor the assurance of a right to recover them at economic rates of production nor assurance as to how long that right will survive, notwithstanding the enormous investment required."[17] If the United States were to sign the UNCLOS treaty, American companies could "be expected to cut their losses and either get out of this business altogether, or rent out their technology to the new masters of the seabed."[18]

Ratiner fears that a future president may sign the convention and that it will be less favorable to America than if the United States joins now and seeks to influence the work of the Preparatory Commission. But even if substantial improvements were attainable, it is' unlikely that the Group of 77 would permit elimination of the central feature of the scheme that makes it objectionable to the West: the creation of a supranational institution with the power to directly tax business enterprise. Unless this feature can be eliminated, the treaty remains fundamentally flawed and contrary to the long-term interests of the West. Moreover, while it is possible that a future president might wish to sign the treaty, it is doubtful that two-thirds of the Senate would ever be willing to vote for it. Finally, if the alternative treaty were functioning successfully, there would be no good reason to accept a less advantageous UN treaty. A preemptive surrender of American interests now does not seem justified given these facts.

UNCLOS supporters dismiss as not fatally burdensome certain provisions of the convention objected to by treaty opponents: uncertainty over contract approval by the Authority's Technical Commission, reservation of a minesite for its "Enterprise," production limits to shield land-based competitors, and mandatory technology transfers.

Controls, Certainty, and Incentives

The conclusion that the UNCLOS regime is basically acceptable has been challenged by a number of mining industry executives and American government officials. Brian Hoyle, deputy director of the Office of Ocean Law and Policy at the Department of State, has stated that the convention fails to create an attractive investment climate and that "no company could afford to invest under the treaty."[19] Representatives of the mining industry have announced that their companies will not proceed with nodule recovery under the treaty due to its technology transfer provisions. Conrad Welling of Ocean Minerals Company (the Lockheed consortium) testified in July 1982 that the mandatory technology provision is "completely unworkable." He reasoned that "thousands of consortium subcontractors own seabed mining technology. It would be impossible to continue its development if subcontractors had to transfer their technology to the Third World."[20] Richard A. Legatski, counsel to the National Ocean Industries Association, argued that "the ability of foreign consortia to operate efficiently would be jeopardized by their participation in the treaty because U.S. companies won't do business with them. Without the technology supplied by American companies it's likely no one will mine the seabed."[21]

Treaty supporters concede that uncertainty over contract approval and other actions of the Authority creates substantial risks. The rules and procedures for choosing private miners have not yet been drafted, but will be written by a Preparatory Commission before the convention comes into force. No one can guarantee that these rules and procedures will be fair or adequate. Representatives of seabed mining nations are likely to constitute only a minority of the Preparatory Commission members. Moreover, the Technical Commission that will choose who can mine has considerable discretion that may be abused.

Some American treaty advocates believe that production limits on seabed mining to protect land-based producers are unlikely to have any effect. Under the treaty, the total output of nickel of all licensed seabed miners may not in any year exceed the sum of the growth in annual world nickel consumption during the five years preceding commencement of seabed mining plus 60 percent of the growth in nickel consumption from inception of seabed mining to the year in question. The existing demand for nickel and the balance of the growth in demand not set aside for seabed miners is reserved for the land-based producers. Should the latter join in a cartel to raise prices or should technological breakthroughs make seabed mining competitive, a treaty signatory would still be prohibited from exceeding these quotas until they expire, twenty years after mining begins.

Zambia, Zaire, and the USSR are currently the principal U.S. suppliers of cobalt, essential for the manufacture of jet engines and nuclear propulsion systems. Besides nickel, nodules recovered from the seabed contain copper, manganese, and cobalt. The convention stipulates that none of these other metals may be taken in seabed mining except insofar as they are by-products of nickel recovery. This limits the opportunity that seabed mining affords the West for access to strategic minerals outside of hostile or unstable political jurisdictions. Third World advocates of the UNCLOS regime argue that one of the treaty's strengths is that it will protect the interests of land-based producers and prevent developed states from meeting their needs for strategic minerals through seabed mining. One G−77 UNCLOS representative writes:

One could not reasonably contemplate creating, through a universal treaty, conditions that guaranteed to any existing consumer country, currently partially dependent on imports of minerals, future self-sufficiency through its participation in seabed activities alone. I am advised that the opinion of the experts is that this is not practical. It would prove unacceptable to the bulk of land-based producers and others who would not permit the "common heritage" to be employed uniquely to meet the needs and interests of one industrialized state or even a group of industrialized states.[22]

Treaty supporters have suggested that the convention's provisions for mandatory technology transfer are more offensive in theory than in practice. The conclusion that this and other objectionable provisions lack operational significance is not supported by the behavior of the parties most affected. If they were superfluous, the Third World would not have resisted their deletion and the mining consortia would not have mounted so tenacious an opposition.

UNCLOS as a Precedent

Although the specific provisions of the UNCLOS mining regime are disadvantageous to the West, it was clearly the treaty's precedential aspects that helped mobilize the coalition that succeeded in blocking its adoption by the United States. To appreciate why a treaty constituting an important first step in establishing the NIEO is disadvantageous, it is necessary to understand what other changes in the world economic system are contemplated by the Group of 77. There is virtually no significant area of the international economy that would not be affected by the NIEO to the detriment of the United States and the West. For instance, the Group of 77 demands that multilateral lending institutions such as the World Bank and the IMF be reconstituted to increase the influence of recipient states and to decrease the authority of the nations that are the source of their funding. These already generous lenders could lose all restraint; loans would be viewed by all as de facto grants; and worldwide inflation would be administered by financial institutions hostile to the West. The Third World demands that international trade be realigned in its favor. The relatively free market existing in commodities and goods and services would be replaced by centrally administered cartels.

Despite the apparent failure of the convention to enter into force and serve the "pioneering" role its drafters intended for it, the form the law of the sea negotiations took has become a paradigm for other multilateral forums. This has been especially evident as political controversies extraneous to the traditional concerns of certain UN agencies have been inserted into their agendas by the Third World in order to create bargaining counters to trade to the West for tangible concessions.

A recent example occurred at a meeting of the International Telecommunications Union (ITU). The ITU is charged with allocating certain radio frequencies and parking spaces for telecommunications satellites in geosynchronous orbit. Western nations developed communications and space technology, and their demand for frequencies and orbital parking spaces is increasing. They want to safeguard their access to resources they have created. The Third World, on the other hand, wants to reserve its "fair share" of these assets for itself. "We are in favor of equitable access to frequencies. It is a natural resource of humankind," said Iranian ITU delegate K. Arasteh.[23] Tommy T. B. Koh, the president of UNCLOS, has asserted that space, like the seabed, is the common heritage of mankind.

At its last session, the Arab states demanded that Israel be expelled from the ITU because of its invasion of Lebanon. "International organizations in the UN family cannot restrict themselves specifically to technical and economic questions," maintained Moureddin Bouhired, the Algerian delegate. The *Business Week* report on the meeting concludes:

Because of political distractions such as the Israeli expulsion vote and the restructuring of the ITU administrative council to weight it with Third World nations, Western countries now launching satellites cannot get the approval needed to plan communications systems and determine the feasibility of their investments.

Rather than initiating changes to protect their longer term requirements, industrialized nations led by the U.S. are on a bargaining treadmill. . . . Western countries view their attendance at ITU meetings as marking time. "If you don't lose you've won" says Richard Crowell of Communications Satellite Corporation.[24]

Conclusion: The Danger to Western Democracy

That the principle of "the common heritage of mankind" should be applied promiscuously would not be so alarming if there were some way fairly and objectively to determine what is in mankind's

interest. However, that determination depends upon the values or
the ideology of those deciding and will be made by organs of the
United Nations composed of the appointees of its large majority of
small, impoverished, and generally undemocratic states. Thus the
outnumbered Western democracies have good reason to fear that
the representatives of these nations will define mankind's common good to consist of what reinforces the tenure of their
oligarchies and is unfavorable to the West.

There is no record upon which to judge the practical effects of
supranational institutional control of an important economic activity. The record of centrally planned economies in individual
states is the closest approximation of the schemes proposed. They
have proved greatly inferior to countries with relatively unfettered market economies. If the extension of central planning to
the management of vast new areas of economic activity results in
inefficiency, corruption, and stagnation, it would not be in the interests of all mankind. There can be no doubt that mankind in the
West would suffer lower incomes than would otherwise have been
true if the sea treaty succeeded or the NIEO gained acceptance.
Moreover, the acceptance of the principles of the NIEO would
undermine democratic capitalism because they deny the legitimacy of the values upon which that system is based. If the
principles contained in the treaty stand unchallenged, if they are
gradually assimilated into Western law and custom, it will become
progressively more difficult to resist their advance.

Few should be surprised that an organ of the United Nations
takes actions opposed by and detrimental to the United States.
The willingness of America in this context to stand against the
tyranny of the majority in the United Nations will strengthen
its hand in multilateral fora and be a prophylactic measure
against the spread of harmful precedents. Refusal to acquiesce
will help to persuade adversaries that American threats not to
participate and to actively oppose UN policies are serious. To sign
a treaty so offensive to basic American values could incite even
more extreme demands upon the West. Appeasement and weak-
ness are not successful tactics in world politics.

If it is the aim of a nation to maintain its prosperity and political
independence, then the NIEO and the designs of Third World
governments upon the rest of the world's resources should be

resisted. This resistance should take place now, and the Treaty on the Law of the Sea should be rejected and its regime opposed by the United States.

5

ROBERT A. GOLDWIN

Common Sense
vs.
"The Common Heritage"

When President Reagan's decision was announced in March 1981 that the United States would not continue negotiations and would instead begin what turned out to be a lengthy review of the Law of the Sea Treaty, proponents of the treaty in the United States and elsewhere in the world were incredulous. Two years later, after completion of the review, after announcement of the "six objectives" that the United States sought and other nations did not agree to, and, finally, after announcement that the United States would not sign the treaty or participate in any future preparations or activities, the proponents of the treaty are still incredulous. They do not believe, they cannot accept the thought, that the United States will not be a signatory.[1]

To them the benefits to the United States, as to the world, seem so obvious that they can offer only three possible explanations for President Reagan's actions: that he is ignorant,[2] that he is a rigid ideologue,[3] or that he is both.[4]

The argument I shall put forth suggests the reverse: it is the critics of the Reagan policy, the *proponents* of the Law of the Sea Treaty themselves, who have allowed unthinking commitment to ideology to blind them to dominant facts that lie at the heart of the controversy over whether to sign the treaty.

Let us turn directly to the questions that matter: What, if anything, is wrong with the treaty? Is there reason not to sign it? If we do not sign, what should we do?

"Law of the Sea" and "Law of the Seabed"

To begin to see what is wrong with the treaty we must make a distinction so obvious that almost everyone either ignores or overlooks it. The treaty deals with two significantly different kinds of subject matter: one has to do with *the sea,* the other with *the deep seabed.* It deals with the former tolerably well, and by acceptably sensible means. The latter it botches incredibly, in ways that are simultaneously excessive, irrelevant, and potentially oppressive. The parts having to do with the sea—fishing, navigation, shipping, pollution control, marine research, and the like—are familiar subjects of international maritime agreements and are properly called "law of the sea." The provisions having to do with the deep seabed, on the other hand, are unprecedented in international agreements; they are an international novelty and should go under a different name, for the sake of clarity and truth: "the law of the deep seabed." These provisions pertain only to the seabed of those waters beyond territorial limits or economic zones of any nation, beyond the continental shelf, and to the nonliving resources lying on the deep seabed. The specific nonliving resource that has been the object of attention of the negotiators for more than a decade has been the manganese nodules, presumably worth billions of dollars, just lying there at great depths, presumably waiting to be scooped, pumped, or sucked up, then to be transported, refined, and sold for immense gains.

This distinction between *the sea* and *the deep seabed* is the essential starting point for understanding what the problem is and what is at stake. *All* of the controversy over whether to sign the treaty centers on the law of the deep seabed, *none at all* on the law of the sea. If the treaty dealt only with the law of the sea, the United States would have signed long ago. If the treaty were now stripped of the deep seabed provisions, and no other word in the treaty were touched, the United States would sign without delay. There are provisions in the sea portions with which the United States is not especially pleased—some having to do with fishing, others with marine research—but on balance the spokesmen of the United States, including especially President Reagan, have expressed themselves repeatedly as not merely satisfied but even pleased with that major part of the text of the treaty.

There is nothing surprising in this. Few other nations have as much of a stake in the law-abiding, peaceful use of the oceans as has the United States. Use of the oceans increased too rapidly in recent decades. As a result, new problems were generated and old ones were intensified. It was obvious that some wholly new rules needed to be formulated, some existing rules needed strengthening, and in certain very important situations long-standing customary rules needed codification. The United States made useful, major contributions throughout these negotiations and was not unhappy with the results. President Reagan affirmed this in his statement announcing that the United States would not sign the treaty. He explained that the provisions dealing with the law of the sea contained "positive and very significant accomplishments." Most of the provisions, he said, "are consistent with United States interests and, in our view, serve well the interests of all nations."[5] In short, the United States would be a willing signatory if the law of the sea were the full subject matter of the Law of the Sea Treaty. But it isn't; the law of the deep seabed is a part of it, too.

It should also be noted that to implement the provisions of the treaty dealing with the principal activities of the world's oceans—fishing rights, navigation and overflight, pollution control, marine research, and similar matters—not one new international agency had to be brought into existence. But everything is quite different when we turn to the other part, the troublesome part of the treaty, the part that deals not with the sea but with the deep seabed and

the inanimate things that rest on it. This part of the treaty an-
nounces a new doctrine of international control, if not international ownership, of hitherto unowned territories, and it establishes new institutions that rival the United Nations itself in size,
scope, complexity, powers, and numbers of employees. There
would be an Assembly, a Council, a Secretariat, a number of expert commissions, courts of various sorts called disputes cham-
bers, and a mining company called the Enterprise that would—on
paper, at least—be equal in size, funding, and activity to all of the
competing private sea-mining consortia of the world *combined*.

Ill-Founded Hopes

The obvious justification for a new law of the sea is the greatly intensified use of the seas by the nations of the world, which gener-
ates new problems that must be addressed in a constructive manner—and which by and large, on balance, have been so dealt with
in the treaty. But what is the justification for the new law of the
deep seabed? The answer given by treaty proponents is that the
manganese nodules present a new problem and a new opportunity
for global development and international economic justice.

To understand the deep seabed provisions of the treaty, it is
necessary to try to recapture the aspirations and expectations of
the negotiators in the 1960s and 1970s. The assumption was that
the manganese nodules represented tremendous riches and that,
unless strict precautions were taken and enforced with energy
and vigilance, only the most wealthy and technologically advanced
nations would profit from this new source of raw materials. This
gave birth to the doctrine of "the common heritage of mankind,"
interpreted to mean that the unowned and unacquired nodules
already belonged to "mankind as a whole" and that each
sovereign nation owned a share of the common property. By
carefully drawn rules to be made, administered, and adjudicated
by novel international agencies, the poorer nations would get a
fair share of the immense profits, would acquire advanced technology, and would assume a new role in actually managing vast
enterprises that would dwarf the most optimistic possibilities in
their own smaller and poorer national economies. It sounds won-
derful but there are two things wrong: the theory and the facts.

Three hundred years ago the argument was made that a "universal commons" (based on a false analogy to the familiar village commons) is impossible. A village commoner can help himself to much of what is common without seeking the consent of his fellow commoners, but the commons itself is property, joint property that excludes others who may not take what they please without permission. There can be no property, no ownership, without excluding others. Where others can take what they want without another's consent, there is no property. In short, to speak of the deep seabed as a universal or "global" commons either is nonsense, literally, or it means that *no one owns the seabed* or anything on it, which is where matters stood *before* the treaty was written.

That the deep seas are unowned has been the principle underlying freedom of the seas for centuries. A doctrine that seems to proclaim that they are now "owned" by "mankind" is used in the treaty to claim the right of an international authority to control and regulate uses of the seas. This theoretical nonsense jeopardizes one of the great foundations of international peace and prosperity—freedom of the high seas.[6]

Not only is the theory wrong, but the factual assumptions underlying the treaty provisions are even more obviously wrong. Some experts probably knew from the beginning that it was all a pipe dream. It was certainly known by many in 1981.[7] For example, in May 1981, spokesmen of the Kennecott Consortium, in a detailed report to the House of Commons, described how calculations based on surveys in the 1950s and 1960s misled mining companies to think that nodules could become profitable, but that "estimates of the total resource of nodules have little significance since they take no account of the economics of recovery," which had been grievously miscalculated. "Only a very small fraction of the total resources of nodules can be classified even as potential reserves—a term that implies that they can be mined profitably." The report contends that the provisions of the treaty are a disincentive for investment in mining, but then adds that "even with no legal, economic, or financial restraints a nodule project is unlikely to be in operation before 1990. Market considerations . . . may postpone the first project even longer." Finally, they say, "Whilst it cannot be denied that the total content of manganese, nickel, copper and cobalt in all the nodules in the oceans may be vast, most of this resource will be uneconomic for many decades—*possibly centuries*" (my emphasis).[8]

Two great errors underlying treaty negotiations were that there were useful minerals lying there for the taking and that production of the metals from the nodules would be profitable. The reality is that obtaining the nodules would be very costly and hazardous, refining the metals twice as costly as retrieving them, and the prospects for return on investment sufficiently dismal to bring almost all operations to a complete halt. But starting as they did from these two massive errors, the proponents decided that great efforts were justified to regulate the increased activity that would develop—that new courts were needed to judge disputes, that commissions were needed to control production and prices, and that legislative bodies with new principles of representation were needed to assure that the wealth that would be pouring in would be shared fairly. Dreams of untold wealth are not a new phenomenon in human history, nor are they easy to give up, but in the case of the nodules there is no alternative.

No Market for Seabed Minerals

The chief minerals in the nodules are manganese, copper, nickel, and cobalt. All have been selling at unusually low prices. For example, the nominal price of nickel in early 1983 was the same as in 1974, despite a decade of high inflation. Manganese is used almost entirely in steel production, and steel production is 50 percent or less of plant capacity around the world, with many steel mills closed down, perhaps forever. Not only are cobalt prices low compared to recent years (about one-fifth of 1979's all-time high), but the volatility of its price and the uncertainty of supply are encouraging consumers to be wary of using it. The Congressional Budget Office (CBO) issued a study urging a review of cobalt stockpiling.[9] The existing stockpile goal is considerably higher than needed, according to the CBO study; it urged that care should be taken not to reduce incentives for development of cobalt substitutes by industry. In short, as *The Economist* wrote of the main ingredients of the deep seabed nodules, "nobody wants these minerals."[10]

Most reports indicate that copper would not be the major factor if there ever were commercial nodule mining, but recent developments in technology make expensive new sources of copper seem even less important commercially. Copper pipe has been replaced by plastics in many applications. Copper wiring is being replaced by fiber optics for much, if not all, of communications traffic. Not only can this glass product take the place of copper wiring, it will provide a new source of scrap copper to compete with copper from land mines or nodules; one analyst contends that the obsolete copper communications cables will be the biggest new reserve of copper in the world. To add to the indignities being heaped on this splendid metal, once so highly prized and profitable, the U.S. Mint now produces annually more than 13 billion pennies that are 97.5 percent zinc (less than half the price of copper), plated with 2.5 percent copper, saving the mint an estimated $25 million a year in metal costs.

Pessimism about the future of many metals seems justified when prices are depressed, but of course those with long experience remind us that prices and profits fluctuate in all commodities, and no one can be sure of the future. The prudential rule, partaking of the character of a natural law, is that whatever goes up must come down, as for example petroleum prices in early 1983 after a decade of huge increases. But nothing in nature or experience says that what is down must go up. The example of copper is instructive. The fluctuations are not simply cyclical or the result of the worldwide recession; the causes are in large part technological innovation and substitution, and of such a nature that, although unforeseen new uses may be developed, some major uses of copper are unlikely ever to return.

Similar dire prospects exist for steel, and (since over 90 percent of manganese is consumed in the steel industry) as steel goes, so goes manganese. The Ford Motor Company says it is testing an automobile with a body made of plastic described as lighter than aluminum and stronger than most steel. KYOCERA Corporation (Kyoto Ceramics) has developed a ceramic diesel automobile engine. It is lightweight, thermal-efficient, estimated to give a 30-percent reduction in fuel consumption, and would practically never wear out.[11] Though one cannot know when or if it will be put into production, an advance model can be driven now. U.S. Com-

merce Undersecretary Lionel Olmer has driven it in Japan and is
quoted as saying, "It's an experimental model and it idles sort of
rough—but it works, that's the main point."

The development of substitutes for metals brings a deep uncertainty that demand, and hence prices, will rise enough (relative to
future prices of everything else) to justify the huge investment
costs of retrieving and refining metals from deep seabed nodules.
Without significant growth of demand, mining nodules for profit
makes no sense. "Production of metals from nodules now would
cost more than from virtually all existing producers and there are
still many undeveloped deposits of these metals on land from
which they could be produced at lower cost than from nodules."[12]

Irrelevance of the Production Provisions

There has always been an internal contradiction in the mining
provisions of the treaty. On the one hand, there was a desire for
production and profit, especially for the Enterprise, to produce the
revenue to sustain the Authority. On the other hand, there was a
powerful tendency to protectionism, to prevent production sufficient to affect adversely the price of minerals from land-mining
countries. A major concern was protection of the prices of the
metals produced by less-developed land-mining countries, heavily
dependent on export income, like "the three Zs"—Zaire, Zambia,
and Zimbabwe.[13] Canada, too, perhaps alone among the developed
nations, was more concerned with devising and enforcing production controls on deep seabed mining than on developing and
facilitating the mining. Canada had in mind, of course, its preemi-
nence in nickel mining. Complicated formulas, practically unin-
telligible even to many experts, were written into the text to em-
power commissions to regulate production and thereby prices.

But in the last few years, without any deep seabed mining,
prices of these metals were affected by a combination of factors—
worldwide recession, inflated dollars, oil price increases, high interest rates, currency fluctuations, energy conservation measures,
discoveries of extensive new land-based mineral reserves, development of substitutes for several metals, and technological ad-
vances—unpredicted but powerful in their effects.

In short, the architects of the treaty thought they were designing protections, through production controls, for price stability in commodities. But the kinds of events that happen all the time in the world economy—and that happen with greater intensity and rapidity in our time than ever before in history—were occurring with a complete disregard for the concerns or the powers of the treaty drafters. The forces at work were, in relation to human law-makers, anarchic; they could not be controlled by anyone's fiat—not by the United Nations, the International Seabed Authority, or solemn words on the heaviest parchment, no matter how many heads of government put their pen to it.

Many proponents of the treaty continue to argue that an inter-national agreement is necessary to give adequate legal security to miners, and that without the treaty it will be impossible for them to get financing for mining operations. Without denying the logic of their argument (and leaving the legal niceties to others who know more about them), I think it sufficient to respond that there will be no financing and no investing in deep seabed mining of manganese nodules for profit in the foreseeable future—"possibly centuries"—with or without the treaty. C. R. Tinsley (in 1981 the vice-president, Mining Division, Continental Bank of Chicago) has written that the treaty's set of mining provisions "brings forth a higher degree of *uncertainty*" (his emphasis) than he had seen in over 250 mining projects worldwide that he had reviewed. His study of the treaty led him to conclude that his bank would not, and probably no bank would, finance deep seabed mining ven-tures. He added:

But if a bank is unwilling to "take" or to absorb certain risks, which it traditionally has been able to do in mine project financings all over the world, then we can be safe in anticipating that the companies themselves are not going to take on these risks either.[14]

This view is borne out by the fact that current work and expen-diture of the mining groups is negligible, and has been for several years now, with no prospect of change.

Some Americans support the seabed provisions for reasons other than profit—for example, for the sake of assured American access to some strategic mineral, or the chance to develop new technology. Such activity would probably be limited, but it would surely produce no revenue such as was dreamed of for sharing with the poorer nations. Profitless mining activity will not sustain the Enterprise, nor will it cover the expenses of the Authority and its hoped-for thousands of employees.

Doubts about Practical Purposes

Where does that leave the law of the deep seabed? It was designed to assert ownership over the nodules, set up agencies to license and regulate their retrieval, resolve the anticipated controversies characteristic of a rush for gold or other precious metals, profit from the Enterprise's sale of the metals, and distribute some of the profits to those who need help most. All of this was to be done from a headquarters financed from license fees and the rest of the Enterprise's profits, for the grand purpose not merely of producing the revenue to support the entire establishment, but especially of taking into its hands, on a supranational basis, the task of aiding the developing world. The aim was to take a giant step in the direction of a new international economic order.

None of these expectations was justified, and none will come to pass. For the foreseeable future there will be no financing (with or without the treaty), no investing, no mining, no licenses, no fees, no disputes to settle, and no contributions from the United States (and no assurance of participation from most of the other nations with a deep seabed mining capability). Thus there is no prospect of funds for the Authority, the courts, the expert commissions, or the Secretariat; no technology or capital to transfer to the Enterprise; and no revenue to share with the poorest countries.

If I am right (and I will, later, consider objections to the argument presented here), a question arises that goes beyond the details of metals and their markets. Why have the proponents of the treaty persisted in trying to have it signed and ratified? That is, if the expected activities are not going to occur, why continue the effort to generate new agencies to guide and control them? If there is going to be little or no production, why persist in establishing the mechanisms to control the levels of production? If the activity will be so limited and the likelihood of disputes so remote, why establish specialized new international courts to adjudicate? If there is going to be no revenue, why continue with plans for an expensive establishment that will be equal to or perhaps greater than the United Nations itself? Why, when there is no practical purpose to serve, do the proponents of the treaty persist?

Unkind answers come immediately to mind. One is that the treaty negotiators have spent a decade and more in a tight world of their own (a world of their own making, one might say) and cannot bear to see it fall short of realization. It would not be the first time that negotiators have become so committed to their own handiwork that they lost touch with the interests of their countries (especially when the matter is of so little interest, as in this case, that few governments have more than a handful, even in the foreign ministry, who know or care anything about the treaty).

Another unkind explanation is concern about careers: many of the diplomats have devoted a major part of their professional careers to the law of the sea. Some of the younger ones have never done anything else. It is *their* subject, their expertise; if the treaty organization does not come into being, they have no way of knowing what other assignment may ever come to them. A test of the validity of this explanation would be to propose one brief addition to the text of the treaty: that no one who has participated in its writing may hold any position of trust in the Authority or the Enterprise or any of its agencies. It is unlikely that such a provision would receive support, but if by some magic it were made a part of the text, support for the treaty would decline sharply among the diplomats. This explanation, I repeat, is unkind, and surely not the basic factor. Nevertheless, diplomats would have to be inhuman for it to be of no significance whatsoever.

There is, finally, an explanation of a different sort that is much more convincing, the one we started with—ideology. Serious professionals who care about the work they do, who are devoted to the principles that guide them and the causes they live for—and that is a fair and accurate description of the proponents of the treaty— do not expend great effort aimlessly. They worked unbelievably hard and very skillfully for a decade to produce the most complex international agreement ever devised. Along the way, either conditions changed or they emerged from obscurity to visibility only gradually. In any case, at some time—sooner for some than for others—all of the competent ones saw that the facts were not as initially described and that expectations were not going to be fulfilled.

In the face of these changes they agreed to some adjustments, but never to any basic ones. They never looked for the elegant reformulations that astute and proud professionals would make if they wished to. When it became clear, for example, that the production-level formulas no longer made sense, they made a "concession" to the United States by changing the formula so that it would have "no bite," but they would not even consider giving up the power to set production levels, nor would they eliminate the commission to exercise that power.

Again, they were willing to make a "concession" that had the practical effect of nullifying the mandatory character of the transfer of technology—but a suggestion that the word "mandatory" be deleted brought only amused smiles that said, in effect, there are some things more important than technology, and the word "mandatory," with all it implies, is one of them.

Again, the text of the treaty provides that the Assembly (not the Council) be the supreme body. Proponents sought to reassure by arguing that many provisions taken together demonstrate that the Assembly (dominated by Third World countries, because they are so numerous) would not really be, for practical purposes, supreme, but suggestions that the text be reworded to accord with their reading of it were not taken seriously.

What can the explanation be for insisting on going forward when no practical purpose would be served? Why, if some provisions for the deep seabed must remain in the text, did the conference refuse to make revisions, deleting unnecessary powers and agencies? The answer is ideology, the ideology of "the common heritage of mankind," the single most sacred of UN sacred cows. If one were to suggest that the deep seabed provisions now be deleted from the treaty, that the remainder—the true law of the sea treaty—be presented for signature and ratification and put into effect, and that the question of the law of the deep seabed be approached separately and anew on the basis of what is now known—if such a proposal were made it would receive the same response as recommendations that India increase its food supply by slaughtering and eating cows, and for a similar reason.[15]

"Common Heritage" vs. Common Sense

If there were no ideological barrier, if the law of the deep seabed could be approached now on the basis of common sense instead of "the common heritage of mankind" ideology, there are several things we could quickly agree on. First, we could agree that there is enough time to proceed sensibly; there is no rush and no crisis. Second, not much, if anything, in the way of new international structures or agencies is required. The level of activity related to the deep seabed will be far less than the activity on the seas, and the agencies and regulatory efforts should be minimal, commensurate to the low level of activity. The private mining consortia have already met; in a very short time they came to an agreement on procedures, by negotiation or arbitration, to settle any disputes that might arise over mining sites. Probably some simple system for registering claims for sites could handle all of the necessary work, since it is estimated that in all international waters there will be no more than five to twenty sites for mining nodules for the foreseeable future. But, most important, there should be no claim put forth of an *inherent right* of an international authority to regulate deep seabed activities.

One of the most fervent proponents of "the common heritage of mankind" doctrine, Elisabeth Mann Borgese, a leader of the world-government movement in the years after World War II (until that movement for global harmony destroyed itself by internal strife among rival world-federalist factions), agrees that ideology is the dominant factor. After listing some developments that have diminished "the value of the Common Heritage of Mankind, particularly of the manganese nodules," she goes on to say that that is not the main point. The main point is that "the creation of the International Seabed Authority . . . must be reckoned as a breakthrough in international relations. Here is an international institution," she writes,

unprecedentedly empowered to regulate and act on the basis of the new principle of the Common Heritage of Mankind. Here is a first attempt at a global production policy with due regard to conservation of the environment. Here is an opening to industrial cooperation between the North and the South based not on aid but on sharing. . . . The International Seabed Authority, a utopian dream of 20 years ago, is now a fact of international law. Something has been moving.[16]

What clearer evidence can there be that for many proponents of the treaty, ideology takes precedence over the explicit practical goals? And if one were to protest that Mrs. Borgese, no matter how devoted and enthusiastic, does not speak for all treaty proponents, we are still left with the puzzle: why, when the stated practical reasons for going forward with the law of the deep seabed have all dissolved, do the advocates nevertheless persist? My answer is that the ideology of "the common heritage" is, as Mrs. Borgese tells us, of overriding importance.

Reasonably Facing the Unforeseeable

I am aware that others might say my analysis is factually wrong, that there are indeed untold riches out there, if not nodules then something else, and that some form of mining and other activities foreseen or unforeseen will indeed occur. Let me turn, then, to these objections.

The very experience I have described teaches that we cannot know what the future will reveal. New discoveries are being made now—for instance, deposits of polymetallic sulfides containing metals in much higher concentrations than in the nodules—and it is considered a certainty that more and richer deposits of nonliving materials will be found in unexpected places and forms not limited to metals. Proponents of the treaty say that for this reason we must be prepared with agencies and regulations to assure an orderly, peaceful, and fair exploitation of the sea's riches, whatever they turn out to be. Without a legal structure, they say, there will be chaos or paralysis: either every claim an occasion for strife and even violence, or no exploitation at all because those who might be active would be intimidated by the uncertainty and danger of an anarchic situation. These, I admit, are valid and formidable objections—but they are answerable.

The attempt to establish elaborate systems and formulae to deal with every detail of the future turned out to be an extravagant waste of time and human talent. The structure was static and the subject matter was fluid. Sensible (rather than doctrinaire) action to bring order to the extraction of raw materials from international waters may be based on several guiding principles:

- use existing international agencies, which are numerous enough already, rather than generate new ones;

- let the regulatory forces be commensurate with the activities to be regulated;

- insist on the principle of encouraging discovery and extraction of materials useful to all, rather than discouraging them;

- encourage nations to cooperate, without unnecessary and complicated international agency interference;

- if nongovernment, for-profit corporations are the ones capable of exploration and extraction, encourage them to function according to their nature and capabilities; and

- assert and impose on others no doctrines that are not necessary for the immediate task (that is, eschew imperious globalism and sweeping claims to powers that are potentially tyrannical).

In short, as an opponent of the present provisions dealing with the deep seabed and as a proponent of the present provisions dealing with the sea, I urge that steps be taken now to make a fresh start. Let the present deep seabed provisions be deleted from the text—Authority, Enterprise, and all. The United States would not delay in signing what would be left: a true law of the sea treaty. The two parts are not naturally linked and are severable; there is no reason why one part should be held hostage to the other. Deliberations could then begin to make simple and brief rules, if and when any are needed, commensurate with the level of activity at the time, utilizing existing entities, aiming to encourage activity, and adding provisions as they might be found necessary.

Provision could be made that a share of profits go to those less fortunate, but to make that possible the rules must be such that profit-making is not only permitted but encouraged. A small office with a dozen or so workers could be established to register claims and to keep records of disputes and their resolution through negotiation or arbitration.

The True Meaning of "Common Heritage"

And what of "the common heritage of mankind"? Can it have no place in new deliberations? My opinion is that a deep seabed treaty is not needed now. If and when one is needed, if the "common heritage" theme is then reintroduced, let us hope that this time, for the first time, it would be considered as seriously and as respectfully as it deserves. It would be a service to rescue "the common heritage of mankind" from the abuse it has suffered at the hands of its ideologues.

The word "heritage" has at least two meanings, one referring to material possessions that are heritable, the other to immaterial principles of good, civilizing truths and wisdom that are handed down from age to age, as expressed in phrases such as "the heritage of constitutional liberty."

Although it would be difficult if not impossible to explain just what sequence of steps led to the false conclusion that all of us have "inherited" the manganese nodules at the bottom of the sea, that meaning of heritage—the material inheritance of property— seems to have dominated the treaty negotiations. This is especially ironic because the initial intention, no doubt, was to elevate our thoughts about the human condition, to encourage us to regard all human beings as equally deserving of treatment as one "kind."

Instead, very quickly, there were enthusiasts speaking of metals as the common heritage, the area to be brought under control of the Authority as "the common heritage area," and the revenue that would flow in as "common heritage dollars." Even today, so high-minded a person as Mrs. Borgese worries about the decline of "the value of the Common Heritage of Mankind, particularly of the manganese nodules." One can see *how* it happened. But *why* do intelligent and principled people collaborate in the debasement of such a splendid phrase and allow thought-polluters to give ugly little rocks lying in the darkest depths of all creation the noble title of mankind's common heritage? Even if the nodules were pure gold, such usage would be desecration.

Mankind's true heritage lies in the great human accomplishments. I mean books, music, plays, paintings, buildings; I mean the search for the truth of things through philosophy, theology, poetry, mathematics, logic—yes, even rhetoric. This is not the place to attempt to describe it, but there is a connection, even a progression, from philosophy (seeking knowledge of the nature of things) to technology (the power to use knowledge to transform nature to improve the human condition). Sever the bond, separate philosophy and technology, and we are left with a defective "heritage," either formless *stuff* or airy abstraction.

Human beings are not capable of "creation," the divine power to make something out of nothing. We are bound to materials; that is why we explore ceaselessly to find them. But one aspect of the best in mankind, what is often called the divine within us, is the striving to make much out of little, progressively making more and more out of less and less. Sometimes the most advanced technology is spoken of as "miraculous," by which we mean that in the admixture of mind and matter, the matter is so lowly and the quantity of it so negligible (e.g., silicon chips from sand) that the combined product is almost immaterial, almost all mind, as if divinely made, just as we tend to call the best poetry or music "heavenly."

If most practical-minded diplomats would consider this a strange approach to useful thinking about the deep seabed, they would be right. But we must not forget that *they* are the ones who introduced "the common heritage of mankind" into the proceedings and never ceased to brandish it thereafter. Their failure to understand what they were talking about explains, at least in part, why a decade of their brilliant work has ended in contention, bitterness, and failure. In my opinion, nothing could be more practical than to reflect on the two different meanings of the "heritage" and to instill into the proceedings, should there be more of them, some of the higher meaning of the word. Let those who are unwilling or unable to rise to that level acknowledge, honestly, that they were never really serious when they used the phrase, and then let them get on with the job without singing anthems to "the common heritage of mankind."

What good might come from serious reflection in treaty deliberations on the human "heritage"? It might remind us that raw materials, whether low-grade ore or high-grade petroleum, are valuable only if we know what to do with them. Raw materials, *in themselves,* are worthless. The ability to reason and imagine, to learn what to do with raw materials, is what is common to us all, is what makes us, equally, all of one "kind." The only true resources are human understanding and the ability to make nature serviceable.

The great error of the treaty negotiators was to speak and think of the *nodules* as "the common heritage of mankind" and to ignore—worse, to shackle—the true heritage all human beings share, the rational power to make the most of what nature gives, for the betterment of all.

III

Practical Differences: Seabed Mining

6

LANCE N. ANTRIM

JAMES K. SEBENIUS

Incentives for Ocean Mining under the Convention

Vast quantities of coal-like lumps called manganese nodules cover much of the deep ocean floor. These nodules contain a rich harvest of copper, cobalt, nickel, and manganese. During most of the century that followed their discovery, this sunken resource remained a scientific curiosity. In the mid-1960s, however, a number of mining consortia began spending large sums to develop the sophisticated technology necessary to lift the nodules and transport them to land for processing. Industrial nations depend on a few, possibly

Both Antrim (Office of Technology Assessment, U.S. Congress) and Sebenius (Harvard University) have served with the United States Law of the Sea delegation and have worked with the MIT modeling team described herein. The personal judgments expressed in this chapter do not necessarily reflect the views of the organizations with which they are or have been affiliated.

unstable, land supplies for these critical minerals; the seabed thus offers the hope of a more secure alternative source. Recently, however, the economic outlook for ocean mining—whether carried out under private, national, or international auspices— does not appear to justify large-scale commercial investments.

The new Law of the Sea (LOS) Treaty sets up an international legal and political regime for ocean mining. In this chapter, we evaluate the commercial prospects for seabed mining under these arrangements. Though a widely accepted LOS Convention contains burdensome features, we conclude that, relative to the likely alternatives, the new regime should provide a stable business environment that will be reasonably conducive to ocean mining once its underlying economic prospects improve.

Origins and Alternatives

Because the richest and most abundant grounds for mining nodules lie outside the limits of any nation's jurisdiction, the question of generally recognized "title" to the nodules has been a thorny one for potential seabed miners and their bankers. In 1970, without opposition, the United Nations General Assembly declared these deep sea resources to be the "common heritage of mankind" and proposed the creation of an international regime that would ensure "equitable sharing by States in the benefits derived therefrom."[1] Furthermore, an enormous increase in the use of the oceans for commercial and military transport, fishing, energy production, and scientific research repeatedly led to frictions and conflicts that pointed up the inadequacies of existing international laws of the sea. To address this situation, the General Assembly convened the Third United Nations Conference on the Law of the Sea in 1973. As an integral part of their agenda, the participants in these mammoth negotiations faced the task of giving substance to the "common heritage" principle.

At that time, industrialized countries that expected to mine the seabed genuinely preferred an international framework over one composed of a few like-minded mining nations. In the early days of the LOS negotiations, they argued strongly for a "Seabed Authority" that would primarily register claims and permit the orderly development of mining. Some revenue from the operations might be shared with the world community in deference to the common heritage principle. In the LOS forum, however, the conditions for seabed mining were tightly linked to renegotiation of the legal regimes covering a spectrum of other ocean uses. Important maritime countries saw these nonseabed issues as crucial.[2] Thus the numerous coastal developing states in particular could exercise bargaining leverage on the resolution of seabed questions. Among the linked issues were the extent of national territorial seas and economic zones, eroding rights of commercial and military navigation, fishing rights, offshore hydrocarbon development, continental shelves, natural and artificial islands, straits, archipelagos, marine environmental protection, and peaceful dispute settlement procedures on all these questions.

At the outset of the LOS negotiations, the principal coalition of Third World representatives demanded that an international body be the sole exploiter of seabed resources. With this idea in opposition to the claims registry concept espoused by most of the industrialized world, negotiations on the subject virtually deadlocked. By 1976, however, conference participants began to coalesce behind a "split-the-difference" conception that became known as the "parallel" system. On one side of the proposed system, private and state organizations could mine, while on the other side, an entity—the "Enterprise"—would be established to mine directly on behalf of the international community. For this compromise to have meaning, it was necessary to ensure that the Enterprise could in fact carry out seabed mining. Among other things, it needed access to mining areas, technology, and finances. Land-based producers of the minerals to come from the sea, moreover, insisted on protection in the form of nodule production limits. Negotiations over these items proved extremely contentious as their burden increasingly fell on the miners who would operate on the "private" side of the parallel system.

Frustrated by the slow pace and inhospitable direction of the LOS talks, the United States in 1980 enacted legislation allowing its companies to proceed unilaterally. Other potential mining nations could join with the United States to set up a "reciprocating states" or "mini-treaty" regime that acted at once as a spur to the LOS deliberations and as a more palatable alternative to an unsatisfactory negotiated outcome. Unhappy with several philosophical and practical aspects of the draft LOS Convention (e.g., the governing system, seabed production limits, mandatory provision of sites and technology to the Enterprise, and so forth), the United States attempted through April 1982 to negotiate substantial changes. While the parallel system provisions of the convention remained largely immune to these efforts, conference delegates did pass a resolution guaranteeing very special rights to "pioneers" in the ocean mining industry.

In April 1982, 130 nations (including France and Japan—both mining states) voted to adopt the resulting convention. The United States and three others cast negative votes while 17 countries abstained, including the seabed mining nations of West Germany, the United Kingdom, Italy, the Netherlands, Belgium, and the Soviet Union.

On 29 June 1982, President Reagan announced that the seabed provisions of the convention, even with the changes and resolutions adopted by the conference, failed to meet the objectives he had established in January, and that therefore the United States would not sign the convention as adopted by the conference. While leaving open the possibility that the United States might sign a convention if further changes were adopted, the president foreclosed the possibility that the U.S. would actively seek such changes.

In December 1982, the draft convention was opened for signature in Jamaica. One hundred seventeen nations (including the Soviet Union, France, and the Netherlands) endorsed the treaty. Japan signed it shortly thereafter. True to the president's word, the United States declined to join.

At least three possible regimes—the full-blown LOS Treaty, unilateral United States legislation, and its possible expansion to a "mini-treaty"—thus confront would-be nodule miners. Each system carries a distinct set of ideological overtones, precedential implications, and linked issues. In this chapter, however, we shall blind ourselves to these important considerations and adopt a primarily commercial viewpoint. We first investigate the economics of an unfettered mining operation, which, in the near to medium term at least, do not seem very promising. We then attempt to gauge the effects of controversial treaty provisions on commercial operators. In comparison to its leading alternatives, we find that when the underlying economic prospects brighten, a widely agreed-upon treaty can offer a reasonably stable though burdensome business environment for ocean mining.

Economics of Seabed Mining

Although mineral deposits exist in many parts of the deep ocean floor, commercial interest centers on nodule deposits located between the Clarion and Clipperton fracture zones, centered about 1,000 miles southeast of Hawaii and 2,000 miles southwest of California. The most promising deposits in the Clarion-Clipperton region contain about 25 percent manganese (essential for steelmaking), 1.4 percent nickel (required for stainless steel), 1.1 percent copper (needed for electrical equipment), and .25 percent cobalt (needed for high-technology alloys and magnets). Deposits of this grade would constitute a remarkable find on land, but at ocean depths of 15,000 feet their economic exploitation would be impossible without extensive research and the development of new mining techniques. Four multinational consortia have carried out this expensive and uncertain work. Two consortia have succeeded in intermittent tests of prototype mining systems. Similar research has been conducted by the governments of France, Japan, India, and the Soviet Union.

It is presumptuous to conduct an evaluation of the economics of an industry that has yet even to complete prototype operations. Still, such analyses must be done by organizations interested in the potential of ocean mining as an investment or as a source of critical materials. This need led the National Oceanic and Atmospheric Administration to fund a research group from the Department of Ocean Engineering and the Sloan School of Management at the Massachusetts Institute of Technology (MIT) to develop a computer model of the costs and profitability of a representative ocean mining operation.[3]

The cost analysis drew upon the patents and general descriptions of ocean mining systems published by the ocean mining industry and upon the much more detailed descriptions of components of the mining systems available from related fields, such as offshore oil development, mineral processing, marine transportation, and scientific exploration. The cost estimates were incorporated into a financial analysis program that would assess the profitability over time of an operation in terms of its discounted cash flow.

The MIT model was developed between 1976 and early 1978. The systems design, costs, and revenue estimates were from the first quarter of 1976. The baseline case of the model showed positive (after tax) net present values at real discount rates up to 18.1 percent. Such rates of return could sustain interest in ocean mining but certainly did not promise a bonanza in view of the risks involved.

Table 1

Economics of Deep Ocean Mining

(cost in millions of dollars, adjusted to 1st quarter, 1981)

	1978		1981
	Baseline	Baseline with modified system design[a]	Baseline
Prospecting	2.4	2.4	5.0
Exploration	22.5	22.5	25.0
Capital cost			
Mining	144.9	218.6	345.9
Transportation	83.8	153.2	221.4
Processing	520.1	598.9	573.5
Total capital	748.8	970.6	1,140.8
Annual operating cost			
Mining	32.1	52.9	71.5
Transportation	22.6	39.6	23.0
Processing	98.0	109.2	122.5
Total operating	152.7	201.7	217.0
Annual revenues	392.4	392.4	424.8
Discounted rate of return[b]	18.1%	10.5%	9.5%

[a]Three changes in the baseline case included in this version of the 1978 model are also found in the 1981 version: use of two mineships instead of one, U.S. built and operated transport vessels, and increased distance of the processing plant from the unloading terminal.

[b]The underlying cash flows imply positive net present values at discount rates— up to the indicated value.

Sources: Authors' calculations from data in J. D. Nyhart, et al., *A Cost Model of Ocean Mining and Associated Regulatory Issues,* MIT Sea Grant Report MITSG 78–4 (Cambridge, Mass.: MIT, 1978); and personal communication with J. D. Nyhart, professor of ocean engineering and management at MIT.

The MIT group revised the model in 1981. Design changes and new cost and revenue estimates, updated to the second half of 1980, were made with the assistance of industry experts. The estimates showed a substantial increase in real costs over those in the original model (see Table 1). As a result of prototype tests conducted in 1979 and 1980, the new model uses more complicated and expensive designs than were believed necessary in 1978. Moreover, the average metal content of nodules in a minesite are lower in the revised model, reflecting the results of later exploration. As illustrated by the changes in the model over the five years from 1976 to 1981, the economic outlook for ocean mining is not particularly good at present and does not promise significant improvement in the near future. These conclusions are generally shared by other researchers.[4] The high costs of ocean mining are due largely to the bulk and complexity of the equipment involved, and there do not seem to be major improvements on the horizon. While it is likely that real metal prices will increase, resulting in an increase in revenues, it is also likely that capital and operating costs will increase. Increases in metal prices would also increase the attractiveness of competing land-based mineral deposits.

These results, of course, do not predict the doom of the ocean mining industry. There is enormous uncertainty in such estimates. If a miner can obtain equipment at a lower cost, for example, if metal prices increase at a relatively higher rate, or if higher-grade deposits are found, ocean mining can represent the new lower cost source for these minerals. If an investor or government places a premium on obtaining direct assured access to a supply of manganese, say, then a lower financial return may be acceptable. Moreover, there may be early entrants who wish to position themselves strategically in the new industry or to develop an advantage in deep ocean technology. Thus, while ocean mining in general does not now seem to be a financially attractive investment, it is plausible in the future that investors may wish to proceed with the enormous commercial-scale investments required for seabed production.

Political and Legal Environment

Investment opportunities in ocean mining cannot be evaluated solely as an exercise in economics but must also include consideration of the political and legal environment. This requires an evaluation of the regime established by U.S. law (and whatever bilateral agreements can be used to supplement it) as well as that of the Law of the Sea Convention and the resolutions of the conference.

United States law. Under the provisions of the Deep Seabed Hard Mineral Resources Act of 1980, an American citizen, corporation, partnership, or other business entity controlled by an American citizen must obtain a license for exploration or a permit for exploitation before conducting ocean mining activities on the seabed beyond the limits of national jurisdiction. Issuance of a license or permit would exclude all other Americans from conducting exploration or exploitation activities within the specified minesite. The conduct of such activities would be subject to domestic environmental and other regulations, and, in addition to normal corporate taxes, miners would be required to pay a tax equivalent to 0.75 percent of the gross revenues from the sales of metals produced from nodules.

The United States legislation can grant exclusive minesite rights only as against other U.S. citizens. For this reason there is a provision for reciprocal recognition of exploration rights issued by other countries that establish compatible ocean mining programs. Through a series of such reciprocal agreements among all potential ocean mining countries it would be possible to eliminate the possibility of conflicting minesite claims.

Law of the Sea Convention. A prime disadvantage of a domestic regime is that it does not provide widespread recognition of an exclusive right to explore and exploit a minesite. One purpose of the LOS Convention is to establish a regime for deep seabed resources that can grant widely accepted exploitation rights and provide for orderly resolution of conflicting claims. This environment would facilitate planning and capital-raising activities.

Unlike the terms of many Third World mineral agreements, early seabed contracts with the International Authority are relatively fixed because the key provisions are written into the treaty itself. Such contractual stability will be attractive to private mining companies, many of whose frequent experiences with expropriation and forced renegotiation have led them to invest in developed countries or a few "safe" developing countries rather than be subject to "political risk" in many countries that have geologically superior deposits.[5]

Nevertheless, miners will encounter a number of financial costs and regulatory uncertainties associated with operating under the LOS Convention. While many of these provisions have stirred much political controversy, their practical effects are likely to be relatively modest. We first discuss the most significant of these and then consider the mitigating effects of the Resolution on Pioneer Investment passed near the end of the 1982 LOS session.

Uncertainty over contract approval and other actions of the Seabed Authority. According to the treaty, all qualified applicants must be issued a contract for exploration and exploitation. A determination of qualification is made by a Legal and Technical Commission according to the rules, regulations, and procedures of the International Authority. This causes two uncertainties for a potential investor. First, the rules, regulations, and procedures have not yet been written, but will be drafted by a Preparatory Commission before the convention comes into force. The second uncertainty is over the predictability and fairness of the actions of the Legal and Technical Commission, which is to consist of experts in the fields related to ocean mining. Commission members are supposed to base their decisions on objective criteria established by the treaty and the rules of the Authority. The commission does, however, possess considerable discretion, and there can be no ironclad assurance except through the treaty's dispute resolution procedures that abuse of this discretion will not occur.

Reservation of a minesite for the Authority. A basic element of the convention is that an applicant for a minesite must propose two areas for exploration and exploitation, one of which will be selected by the Authority and reserved for the Enterprise. This requirement increases the effort that must go into prospecting the seabed for exploitable deposits, but the costs involved (almost certainly less than $10 million) are small with respect to the billion-plus-dollar capital costs required for an operation.

Financial payments to the Authority. The greatest burdens for a miner operating under the convention regime are the financial payments that must be made to the Authority. The convention provides alternative systems of determining the payments required. One system, a simple royalty payment based on gross revenue from the sale of metals from nodules, is included for use primarily by the centrally planned economies such as the Soviet Union's that do not calculate profits. A second system, which combines a reduced royalty with a profit-sharing system, is favored by market economy countries.

The financial provisions of contracts are designed to function well in the risky environment of ocean mining.[6] Operators pay a base royalty equal to 2 percent of gross revenues and 35 percent of any mining profits. For projects that are extremely successful, payments include a 4 percent royalty and a 70 percent share of the marginal profit dollar from mining operations during later years of the operation. (There is also a series of intermediate rates.) Two things should be kept in mind about these figures. First, all financial calculations are done in constant (deflated) terms, implying that only real profits are taxed—not paper profits, as is common under domestic law. Second, while rates such as 70 percent may appear high, they apply *only* to the mining portion—about 25 percent—of an integrated project, and then *only* to the highest profit increment after a significant discounted cash flow return has been reached by the entire project. Thus the maximum effective marginal tax is 17.5 percent—equal to a 70 percent rate applied to 25 percent of the net profit of an integrated operation. The highest rate takes effect only late in the life of a very successful project. By similar reasoning, the base tax rate is 8.75 percent of the net profits of an integrated operation.

The magnitude and nature of payments made under the convention compare favorably with those made in many developing countries by land-based mining operations, but, unlike many such terms, the LOS rates are not in practice renegotiable upwards.[7] While the seabed payments may be substantial, their effects are somewhat mitigated by the progressivity of the tax system (see Table 2). In addition, the financial burden on investors can be greatly reduced if the investor's parent government allows all or part of the payments to be credited against its taxes.

Table 2

Effect of Revenue Sharing on Profitability

Case[a]	Discounted rate of return with revenue sharing	Discounted rate of return without revenue sharing[b]	Decrease
A	2.6%	1.1%	1.5%
B	5.0	3.4	1.6
C	9.5	7.8	1.7
D	16.3	14.0	2.3
E	19.1	16.5	2.6
F	25.4	22.2	3.2

[a]All cases are based on the cost and revenue estimates of the 1981 revision of the MIT model and assume that international payments are deductible against U.S. taxes.

Case A: 25 percent increase in capital and operating costs

Case B: 25 percent increase in operating cost

Case C: Baseline case for 1981 revision

Case D: 25 percent increase in revenues

Case E: 25 percent increase in revenues, 10 percent decrease of capital and operating costs

Case F: Same as Case D with 2.5 percent annual increase in metal prices

[b]All underlying cash flows imply positive net present values at discount rates up to the indicated value.

Sources: Authors' calculations from data in J. D. Nyhart, et al., *A Cost Model of Ocean Mining and Associated Regulatory Issues,* MIT Sea Grant Report MITSG 78–4 (Cambridge, Mass.: MIT, 1978); and personal communication with J. D. Nyhart, professor of ocean engineering and management at MIT.

Production limits. The convention will establish a fifteen-year limit on the annual production of seabed nickel. While the principle of a production limit has drawn much criticism, in practice it is unlikely to have much effect. The limit is calculated as the sum of the growth of nickel consumption over the five years prior to the first commercial mining operation plus 60 percent of the growth of nickel consumption thereafter. To protect against exaggerated restrictions during periods of low market growth, the treaty imposes a 3 percent growth rate "floor" for the calculation. Table 3 shows the range of allowable production under the limit, based on a plausible starting date of 1995 for the first mining operation and future growth rates of world nickel consumption that encompass the pessimistic, likely, and optimistic cases projected by the U.S. Bureau of Mines.[8] Although these estimates are uncertain, they do establish a lower bound to the probable number of available minesites.

Table 3

Effect of the Production Limitation on Deep Ocean Mining

(nickel production in thousands of metric tons per year)

Year	2.4% Annual growth rate		3.0% Annual growth rate		4.0% Annual growth rate	
	Nickel production	Minesites	Nickel production	Minesites	Nickel production	Minesites
1995	177.4	4.6	200.6	5.2	268.8	7.0
1996	206.6	5.3	254.2	6.5	345.8	8.9
1997	221.4	5.7	250.8	6.5	357.2	9.2
1998	244.6	6.3	272.0	7.0	398.0	10.3
1999	255.6	6.6	272.0	7.0	412.1	10.7
2000	268.1	6.9	299.4	7.7	439.5	11.4
2001	312.6	8.1	321.3	8.3	495.9	12.8
2002	342.9	8.9	347.1	9.0	538.5	13.9
2003	367.2	9.5	373.7	9.7	582.8	15.1
2004	391.9	10.1	401.1	10.4	628.9	16.3

Note: Estimates are based on projected nickel growth from a 1979 nickel trend line value of 749 thousand metric tons. Annual production of minesite estimated at 38.7 thousand metric tons of nickel. Number of sites may be higher since some operations will produce manganese while reducing their annual nickel production to approximately 13 thousand metric tons.

Source: Authors' calculations using data from the U.S. Bureau of Mines and Metallgesellschaft A.G.

Based on these projections, on the uninspiring economic forecasts for early ocean mining, and on the small number of prospective entrants, it is quite likely that the production limit will have little practical effect with the possible exception of the first five years. Then, however, pioneer investors would all be allowed to apply for production authorizations under the special conference resolution discussed below. Ironically, the low-growth scenarios in which the production limit could "bite" are those that imply the worst underlying economic climate for the industry, and hence should cause the least worry about the production restrictions.

Technology transfer. Provisions mandating the sale of technology from the private miner to the Enterprise and to developing states have aroused the greatest opposition of all of the convention's provisions. In large part, these objections draw force from the principle that technology should be sold only at the owner's decision and then on freely negotiated terms. As with the production limit, however, the technology transfer provisions in practice are unlikely to have a significant effect.

The treaty forbids the Enterprise to invoke the mandatory transfer obligation unless and until it has failed to obtain the technology by other means, including tenders for bids. Beyond tenders, the Enterprise has other highly potent but noncoercive means at its disposal. Its problem will be less that of prying technology from reluctant owners than of choosing from among the many eagerly proffered systems. Under the financial provisions of the treaty, member governments promise to supply the Enterprise with funds sufficient for an entire integrated project. This amount of money will be at least two or three times the total spent to date by all existing consortia in developing their systems and should more than suffice for the Enterprise to contract for and build its own system, if desired. Some consortia, however, may wish to spread their development costs by licensing their techniques. Moreover, a contract study by the Interior Department indicates that there is a relatively large number of suppliers for every component of an ocean mining system as well as for the design and construction of the system itself.[9] Beyond outright purchase, the Enterprise may also acquire needed technology under a joint venture arrangement, for which it can offer strong inducements.

In the very unlikely event that purchase and joint arrangements fail, any mandated sale must take place on "fair and
reasonable commercial terms and conditions." If the terms offered
by the miner are challenged by the Enterprise or developing countries, then the dispute can be referred to commercial arbitration
for resolution.

There are, however, inhibiting aspects of the transfer provisions. Firms that supply technology not available on the open
market must provide written assurance of their willingness to
negotiate the sale of the technology to the Enterprise. Failure to
live up to this assurance would probably bar the supplier from
future ocean mining operations, but would not affect contracts
that were already approved.

It is worth noting that these potential technology transfer
obligations do not apply to transportation or processing. They apply only to mining technology, the proprietary parts of which
make up significantly less than a third of an operation's capital
cost. Moreover, the entire requirement expires ten years after the
Enterprise has begun commercial production. Hence the overall
practical effects of this obligation, if not its possible philosophical
and precedential implications, are likely to be modest.

Joint ventures with the Enterprise. In addition to the private side
of the parallel system, the convention provides the opportunity for
the Enterprise to enter into joint venture agreements with private
firms. Joint venture operations may be particularly attractive
during the early years of exploitation. At that time, before ocean
mining technology is proven in full-scale operation, private firms
might find investment capital hard to acquire. The Enterprise, on
the other hand, will have no experience in ocean mining and its investment capital will be sufficient to finance only one minesite. A
joint venture would offer advantages to both parties. The private
investor would acquire a partner with low-cost investment capital
that must be used to finance ocean mining. The investor would
also be able to negotiate for financial incentives and reduction of
requirements for banking of sites and technology transfer. The
Enterprise would gain access to the technical and managerial
skills of firms already involved in ocean mining, thereby reducing
the risk of failure due to inexperience and speeding the entry of

the Enterprise into commercial exploitation. In addition, the Enterprise would be able to spread its investment capital over several projects so as to reduce the risk of loss.

Resolution on Pioneer Investment. In addition to the convention, which establishes the future mining regime, the conference adopted a resolution to deal with ocean miners who have already made substantial investments toward nodule recovery. The purpose of the resolution is to provide the stability and certainty necessary to encourage continuation of development activities already under way.

The resolution requires the Preparatory Commission to recognize the exclusive right of a pioneer investor to conduct exploration activities on its minesite. Further, the commission must accept the application of every pioneer investor. Before submitting an application for a site, the pioneer investors must resolve overlapping claims. If conflicting claims cannot be resolved through negotiation, then they will be brought to arbitration based on principles of equity that appear acceptable to industry members.

Investor fears about possible actions by the Legal and Technical Commission should largely be mitigated by the requirement that the Authority approve applications for mining contracts submitted by pioneer investors. The commission can only ensure that the applications are filed in accordance with the convention and the rules of the Authority. In this way, the discretion of the commission will be severely curtailed.

The constraining effects of the production limit could plausibly occur only during the first five years of commercial production. While such a case is unlikely, the resolution establishes procedures for the allocation of production authorizations, if requests exceed the allowable allocation. In this case the authorizations are issued in order of the date of application, except for the Enterprise's first application, which will be given priority. If two or more applications are received at the same time, the applicants must attempt to negotiate a settlement. If negotiations fail, then a decision will be made, probably by the Council, in accordance with criteria specified in the convention and the resolution.

Review conference. Fifteen years after the first operation has successfully tested its systems and has started commercial nodule production, the convention requires that a conference be convened to evaluate the workings of the parallel system. This review conference has five years to decide what changes, if any, should be adopted. If consensus is not achieved by the end of this period, alterations to the system may be made by a three-fourths vote. If, as seems likely, ocean miners begin commercial production in the mid-1990s, the review conference would be convened sometime between 2010 and 2020. This review would present the United States government with the potentially unpleasant prospect of either (1) being bound by the uncertain results of this procedure without formal Senate reconsideration or (2) withdrawing from a treaty that, by then, would be accepted as beneficially governing a wide range of ocean uses other than nodule mining.

As long as a contract is signed, however, between the entry into force of the LOS Treaty and the end of the review conference, Article 155 of the convention provides that the rights under the contract over the life of the mining operation will remain unaffected by actions of the review. Thus, investment decisions that result in contracts issued before the end of the review conference are immune from the effects of future changes.

This period of stability (for the contract, the mining provisions of the treaty, and, effectively, the accompanying rules and regulations) compares favorably with that in many developing country mining agreements, which are constantly subject to the possibility of renegotiation or expropriation.[10] Even in developed countries where investment conditions are usually regarded as stable, taxes and environmental and safety regulations are subject to unpredictable changes—witness the dramatic increase in North Sea oil tax rates as well as the imposition of a windfall profits tax and the reduction in the depletion allowance in the United States. The LOS Treaty provisions, however, are effectively frozen in those respects. Thus, relative to mining regimes on land, the LOS regime offers a stable investment climate for operations commencing before the end of the review conference and producing through the mid-twenty-first century. After that, the terms facing prospective miners will be determined by the results of the review and the countries' reactions to them.

Evaluation

Seabed mining is caught in a larger argument over the Law of the Sea Treaty. Although the interests of the ocean mining industry were cited as a major reason for United States opposition to the draft convention, it appears that the domestic ocean mining industry in particular is now in an ambiguous position.

In light of the large number of countries that have signed the LOS Convention, it is quite probable that the convention will come into force shortly after the Preparatory Commission has completed its work. If at that time the United States still chooses to stay outside the convention, the existence of two separate legal regimes will force American investors to choose among three options. They could (1) push forward under U.S. law as augmented by other states in a mini-treaty, (2) move their operations to a nation that becomes party to the convention, or (3) withdraw altogether from ocean mining activities.

Mining under a unilateral or mini-treaty regime. Operating under U.S. domestic law offers several advantages to U.S. companies. First, the law and regulations relating to it have been drafted with substantial concern for the interests of the ocean mining industry. Second, past experience with the conduct of resource management programs by the government gives potential investors reasonable confidence that the ocean mining program will be carried out efficiently and fairly. Finally, if changes are needed in the program or if government actions are too burdensome, the ocean mining industry is in a position to press for changes.

While the advantage of operating a seabed minesite under domestic law is the certainty about how it will be enforced, the disadvantage is the uncertainty over the value of the rights recognized by the law. The right to mine is exclusive only with respect to other U.S. miners or miners of reciprocating states. Claims could be challenged by any miner that operates under the convention, including France, Japan, the Soviet Union, and India. In addition, the right to conduct any exploration or exploitation activities outside the treaty regime may be challenged by nonseabed mining countries, either individually or collectively. In fact, Ambassador Tommy T. B. Koh of Singapore, president of the LOS Conference, announced that if a mini-treaty among seabed mining countries is established, he will ask the UN General Assembly to refer the question of legality of mining the seabed to the International Court of Justice for an advisory opinion.[11] There is also uncertainty as to which other countries may be able to participate with U.S. citizens. When a country signs the convention, it is bound to recognize the convention regime as the only legitimate one for seabed exploitation. The provisions of the Resolution on Pioneer Investment will temporarily allow signatories to work with nonsignatories until the convention comes into force. At that time, ratifying countries must forbid their citizens to operate under laws of nations that do not sign the convention. This could cause severe, possibly fatal, strains on the mining consortia by forcing companies to change nationality, withdraw from the consortia, or buy out the U.S. participants and apply under the convention.

The disincentive to investment might be significantly decreased if mining consortia could obtain political risk insurance, loan guarantees, or other financial protection from the losses that could result from the United States' being outside the convention. If such protection were made available, it is likely that it would be available only to the United States participants in the consortia. As such, political risk protection would probably be attractive only to the consortia with majority participation by U.S. companies.

The possibility of dispute over exclusive rights to a minesite, the lack of agreed provisions for the resolution of such conflicts, and the threat of international legal action combine with the extremely large capital investment and long payback period to make ocean mining solely under domestic law relatively unattractive. The situation improves to the extent that other mining nations can be persuaded to establish a mini-treaty for seabed exploitation. To be fully effective, such a treaty would need to include all potential ocean mining countries (United States, United Kingdom, Federal Republic of Germany, France, Japan, Netherlands, Belgium, Italy, Canada, USSR, and India) as well as a sufficient number of small industrialized countries and developing states to weaken the support for the convention. The fewer the states participating in a mini-treaty, the greater the opportunity for conflict, delay, and harrassment by outside parties. It is quite conceivable that banks and large corporations would find such risks too high to justify the investments required for commercial-scale operations.

Mining under the convention. Mining under the treaty could offer a higher degree of certainty with respect to the right to mine. While the possibility of conflicting claims with miners operating under U.S. law would exist, the threat of other international challenges from the seabed miners operating under the treaty and from nonseabed mining countries would be eliminated. Even the problem of site conflict with nontreaty miners may be reduced through agreement outside of official channels. Other uncertainties, notably over the approval of mining contracts and the issuance of production authorizations, would be largely eliminated for early investors by the Resolution on Pioneer Investment.

The principal disadvantages to operating under the treaty, in addition to the possibility of conflicting minesite claims, would be the financial costs of prospecting a site for the Enterprise and the payments required under the financial terms of contracts. These burdens could be lessened if the miner's parent country allowed direct credit of the financial payment against its national taxes. Beyond these specific concerns, however, there is always the generalized worry that dealings with an inexperienced international seabed bureaucracy would involve costly delays and obstacles, despite the safeguards in the convention. These could be exacerbated to the extent that land-based producers or others hostile to seabed mining would be able to exert effective cross-pressures on the Authority.

Industry decisions in the short term. Until the work of the Preparatory Commission is complete and the convention comes into force, ocean mining companies will need to protect their options. The most important uncertainty concerns whether the United Kingdom and the Federal Republic of Germany will become parties to the convention. If the United States were isolated outside a convention regime, mining under domestic law could involve real liabilities. If West Germany and Great Britain support the United States regime, then it may be possible, though risky, to conduct operation under a reciprocating states regime. In either case, the best short-term industry decision is to apply for recognition of minesite claims under the domestic regimes of Great Britain and West Germany and thus be ready to operate in whatever regime those countries choose. Two of the four consortia have filed for recognition in those countries through their nationals in the consortia.

The parent countries of all the non-American partners in two consortia have not enacted ocean mining legislation. These consortia could plan to mine under United States law or encourage the parent countries of their non-American partners to pass ocean mining legislation as a bridge to the convention regime.

United States firms could also bypass uncertainties over the legal regime by acting as service companies for other miners. By proper negotiation of a service contract, a company might obtain the benefits of mining under the convention even though its parent country was not a party to it.

The views of private investors on the question of whether the United States should continue to participate in the LOS process depend to a great degree on whether they believe that the U.S. would actually provide risk insurance, loan guarantees, and subsidies to encourage mining outside the convention. A mining company could hedge its bets by lobbying for the United States to remain outside the convention and to provide financial incentives. If attractive enough inducements were made available, the investor could mine under the domestic regime. Otherwise, its operations could be moved to a signatory of the convention.

Conclusions

For straightforward economic reasons, deep ocean mining is not likely to commence for several years. When the economic outlook improves, investment decisions will be greatly affected by questions over the legal right to exploit deep ocean resources. A domestic or mini-treaty regime can go part of the way toward granting that right, but substantial uncertainties will remain. A widely accepted LOS Treaty would assure the right and eliminate most conflicts. The price of such international certainty would be banked sites, financial payments, limited production, technology transfer, and related convention requirements. Any number of grounds exist for objection to these terms. But our comparison of their strictly *commercial* effects suggests that significant deterrence of ocean mining is unlikely to occur, at least through the first two decades of the next century.

7

LEWIS I. COHEN

International Cooperation on Seabed Mining

The Law of the Sea Treaty signed in December 1982 has done nothing to create the confidence necessary to make seabed mining a reality. On the other hand, individual governments have taken concrete actions to protect their interests. Six major industrialized nations (the Federal Republic of Germany, the United Kingdom, the United States, Japan, the USSR, and France) have enacted domestic legislation on seabed mining; others are in the process of legislating. In every case that legislation includes authority for international agreement on mutual recognition of the minesites of other nations. In pursuing this recognition, seabed mining states will construct a framework for avoiding conflict over oceans

This paper was prepared for and delivered during the Seventh Annual Seminar of the Center for Oceans Law and Policy of the University of Virginia School of Law. Copyright © 1983 by the Center for Oceans Law and Policy. The judgments presented in this article are the author's and do not necessarily represent those of the United States Department of State or other agencies of the U.S. government.

resources. Had the seabed mining provisions of the UN treaty been realistic, the U.S. and other Western seabed mining states would not have had to move on their own to create an environment conducive to the multibillion-dollar investments needed to transform remote deposits of seabed minerals into competitively priced industrial materials.

As the Third United Nations Conference on the Law of the Sea (UNCLOS III) unfolded and its Part XI became the plaything of the architects of the so-called New International Economic Order (NIEO), it became clear that the conference was producing a seabed mining text more likely to shackle than to encourage the mining entities of industrialized countries. The conference rode roughshod over the goals of developed Western nations with respect to seabed mining, which were principally:

• open and assured access to any legitimate applicant;

• universal recognition of the right to mine a specific area of the sea floor; and

• security of tenure on that site.

The text encumbers miners' rights with an institutional structure so biased as to cause all but the most enthusiastic supporters of seabed mining to wonder whether the manganese nodule is more political plaything than future resource.

As the Committee I negotiations proceeded, the conference demonstrated that it was not ready to provide either open and assured access on a nondiscriminatory basis or security of tenure. With the emergence of the Informal Composite Negotiating Text (ICNT) in 1976, the basic processes by which the conference could develop a text were called into question. The ICNT, and ultimately the treaty itself, hindered access by failing to provide a reasonable method for the awarding of contracts. The regulatory procedures that were spelled out in the text were prejudicial; other critical seabed mining rules and regulations were left to a Preparatory Commission whose approach could be little different from that of the conference itself. As a result, no business could in good conscience invest $100 million or more of its shareholders' money to explore a site and develop technology knowing that it was dependent on the approval of an institution enervated by an antiproduction, antibusiness bias.

U.S. Mining Law

In these circumstances it is not surprising that the international consortia engaged in seabed operations sought to protect their interests by pressing governments for national legislation. The advocates of national mining laws had various motives. First, many in the United States government, including the delegation to UNCLOS III, thought that the legislation would make clear the U.S. determination to engage in seabed mining and thus might convince those in the LOS Conference to move toward a more reasonable regime. For the most part, these were people who favored a universally acceptable treaty. Second, there were some who thought that domestic legislation would provide an alternative to the treaty should the UN negotiations break down or produce an unacceptable text. This group included many who were skeptical about the ultimate likelihood of a treaty acceptable to both the United States and the Group of 77. Finally, there were some, concerned about our dependence on unreliable sources of supply of strategic materials, who supported the legislation largely because assured access to seabed minerals would ease U.S. dependence on imported strategic materials.

With the unanimous support of the seabed mining industry and the executive branch, Congress passed the Deep Seabed Hard Mineral Resources Act of 1980 (PL 96–283), which provided for American-flag seabed mining that could operate under a law of the sea treaty or other international arrangement, or that could stand on its own were that to become necessary. The statute was important because it was the first explicit legislative sanction by any government for seabed mining.

The provisions in the U.S. legislation that enabled it to act as a bridge to a future UNCLOS III regime were not unqualified. In Section 201, Congress stated its intent that any international agreement to which the U.S. becomes a party should "provide assured non-discriminatory access under reasonable terms and conditions" and provide "security of tenure" by allowing pioneer operators to continue operations without the addition of significant new economic burdens. It is no secret that in the view of the Reagan administration these conditions have not been met by the LOS Convention and that a majority of Congress, and certainly enough senators to block ratification, share this view.

Section 118 of the statute provides the basis for the development of an alternative regime. The executive branch is authorized to negotiate agreements necessary for reciprocal recognition of mining rights. In return for U.S. recognition of foreign minesites, Section 118 requires that foreign governments respect U.S. licenses and permits, comply with certain dates, and develop compatible regulatory programs, particularly in the areas of environmental protection, safety of life and property at sea, conservation of resources, and effective enforcement. Designation of a reciprocating state could occur when these standards were met. The U.S. legislation was quickly followed by a West German law in 1980; Great Britain and France followed suit in 1981. In 1982 Japan and, surprisingly, the USSR enacted essentially similar legislation. Seabed mining legislation in Italy and possibly Belgium is likely in the near future.

Reciprocating States Agreement (RSA)

The U.S. legislation provided not only the authority but also the impetus to consult and negotiate with other countries to establish a general framework for reciprocal recognition of national seabed mining licenses, and such consultations have proceeded with very few breaks since late summer 1980.

The U.S. began the Reciprocating States Agreement (RSA) discussions by providing texts elaborating our views to other delegates in the so-called "like-minded" group of eight nations (West Germany, U.K., France, Belgium, Netherlands, Italy, and Japan). The like-minded group generally reacted favorably, explaining their concerns, seeking modifications, and raising new issues. At each meeting a new draft, more precise and more detailed, would be circulated (almost always by the U.S.). This procedure worked quite smoothly and produced a nearly completed RSA by the end of 1981.

Although those negotiations were conducted privately, word of the meetings seeped out almost immediately to the trade press, to the Law of the Sea Conference, and to the UN Secretariat. It is impossible to specify either the direction or the extent of the influence these meetings had on the conference, although it was a topic often raised by foreign delegates in their informal discussions with U.S. delegates. It was clearly on the minds of many conference delegates in regional group caucuses and informal behind-the-scenes coordinating meetings as they sought to deal with the Reagan administration's position on the UNCLOS III treaty.

By January 1982, on the eve of the eleventh session of the Law of the Sea Conference, four countries having legislation appeared on the verge of signing an RSA. While there was last-minute wrangling over the final text of a related declaration concerning limits on numbers of minesites per country, this was not a major stumbling block. Unfortunately an agreement was not signed at that time. In great measure this was due to differences within the U.S. government between those who felt that signing a Reciprocating States Agreement would leave the U.S. open to charges of bargaining in bad faith at the climactic March-April 1982 session of the LOS Conference and those who argued that an RSA could only strengthen the U.S. hand at the final session by demonstrating political unity among Western seabed mining countries. There can be little doubt that the U.S. failure to sign the RSA reduced the negotiating leverage of each of the four potential parties to it.

Despite the failure to sign a Reciprocating States Agreement in 1982, the months of consultations had a number of beneficial results. Many issues that seemed routine to the U.S. regulatory officials proved not to be routine or even normal under European law. For example, the extensive procedural protections and the limited discretion allowed administrative officials under U.S. law are not reflected in the European legislation, where, for instance, much greater discretion is given to the relevant minister to reject seabed mining applications on fairly broad foreign policy grounds. Impelled by legislation to achieve compatible national approaches to seabed mining, the U.S. delegation had to develop a delicately balanced framework that would influence European administrative policies without dictating the details of individual regulatory programs.

Aftermath of RSA Negotiations

The negotiations to establish reciprocity produced much coordination among seabed mining states. Over time common understandings on the regulatory framework to govern the seabed mining industry have emerged. The U.S. was able to air many of the most vexing problems that it faced in developing a domestic legal regime for seabed mining. The impact of this approach was particularly evident, for example, in the manner in which preenactment explorer license applications were handled. The ultimate solution reflected the views of officials from several nations.

During and after the eleventh session of UNCLOS III, new approaches to the Reciprocating States Agreement were necessary. The other negotiating partners wished to retain the possibility of participating in the system set forth in Resolution II of the LOS Treaty—preparatory investment protection (PIP). The need to "keep options open" meant that a different text would be necessary if the United States were to reach a formal understanding with its partners in seabed mining. Taking into account the new factors in the political equation and elements of the January 1982 RSA text, the U.S. delegation negotiated an agreement limited to conflict resolution. The agreement was signed in Washington by the U.S., U.K., West Germany, and France on 2 September 1982. It features:

- a definition of who will be a preenactment explorer for purposes of conflict resolution;

- procedures for international arbitration of overlapping claims among preenactment explorers;

- specifications of equities to be used by arbitrators in resolving overlapping claims;

- provisions for exchanging information on applications; and

- provisions for further consultations on issuance and recognition of licenses.

The 2 September agreement did not provide for reciprocal recognition of licenses. However, by beginning formal coordination among the seabed mining countries and specifying the rights and obligations that would flow from such recognition, it was a step forward. It also represented a commitment to close cooperation outside the treaty framework, at least until it becomes clear that one or more of the parties will ratify the treaty.

Industry Arrangements

During 1981, the seabed miners began parallel discussions as efforts by their governments to reach agreement continued. The industry sought steady progress on the technical aspects of reciprocal recognition and movement toward an agreed conflict resolution scheme. Early on, the industry had begun internal negotiations to develop arrangements for resolving disputes over conflicting claims. Not surprisingly, the miners soon ran into problems resembling those the government negotiators had encountered. The industry seemed to have concurred with their governments' view that an attempt at private resolution should precede formal government procedures. Since both procedures would depend in part on similar principles, the industry negotiators were forced to keep their discussions ahead of the intergovernmental consultations.

As a result, the industry succeeded in signing an arbitration agreement before the completion of an analogous intergovernmental agreement. Elements of the industry agreement, in particular the equities to be used by the arbitrators, were incorporated into the government text. The industry conflict resolution system is in fact two agreements among the five consortia that filed applications for seabed mining licenses in March 1982 in France, Germany, the U.K., and the U.S. First there is an agreement covering the exchange of information to allow identification of conflicts—the so-called confidentiality agreement. The industry also has an agreement covering the actual resolution of conflicts. That agreement allows for a period of negotiation. If the negotiation fails, procedures are provided for a compulsory and binding arbitration.

The arbitration agreement, applying to all then existing applications for seabed mining licenses, was signed by four multinational consortia on 22 February 1982, with the French consortium, AFERNOD, acceding on 31 March. The confidentiality agreement was signed, and geographical coordinates of each consortium's exploration site applications were shared, on 13 July 1982, permitting the identification of overlapping applications. With conflicts identified, the industry decided that negotiated settlements would be far less expensive and must faster than arbitration. They appear to be making good progress toward voluntary resolution, and no arbitration may be necessary, although this is still uncertain.

The industry agreement did not include the Japanese national consortium, DORD, established in September 1982. However, by January 1983 the other consortia had begun discussions with the Japanese national consortium with a view to including it in the existing system. The inclusion of the Japanese could produce an agreement among all existing seabed mining consortia with claims in the Pacific Ocean.

It would be naive to expect that the American decision to remain outside the LOS Treaty has either smoothed or shortened the path leading to actual exploitation of the seabed. But it is highly significant that the major seabed mining countries are negotiating with the U.S., albeit with an eye on the imperatives of the UN treaty process. The United States cannot accept language in an agreement that commits it to respect a mining regime it finds unacceptable. However, it is likely that the attractiveness of the commonsensical RSA will increase as the LOS mining system becomes better defined. For the moment, however, the seabed mining countries are involved in an intricate gavotte, dancing gingerly to the conflicting rhythms of RSA and PIP.

Guarantees under the LOS Treaty: PIP

The resolution on preparatory investment protection was adopted by the LOS Conference on 30 April 1982. It was intended to draw the seabed mining companies into the treaty system by guaranteeing them exclusive mining rights for specific sites. In some important ways PIP mimics the industry scheme and the conflict resolution agreements the U.S. worked out with the like-minded countries. For example, the equities for an arbitrator to use in resolving a claim are almost identical. Similarly, the requirement to take disputes to binding arbitration after a period of negotiation was a concept developed in the like-minded discussions.

However, PIP is defective in a number of respects. It contains unrealistic timetables, it does not provide an effective means of assuring that applications from bona fide pioneers are approved, and it mirrors many of the defects of the U.S. treaty (via burdensome financial liabilities, and technology transfer and training requirements). Nor does the resolution offer the security of tenure or the assurances concerning contract approval that its supporters asserted were its goal. The resolution did not persuade any of the seabed mining nations with seabed mining statutes that it provides certain access to seabed resources.

Canada has organized a group to discuss conflict resolution procedures under the PIP resolution. Although the Canadians did not "disinvite" the U.S., they made it clear that there was little point in U.S. attendance at their meetings. The Canadians proposed a memorandum of understanding that would create a conflict resolution mechanism providing for the deposition of site coordinates with a registrar, a meeting of states to identify conflicts, and a period for voluntary resolution followed by arbitration under UN Commission on International Trade Law procedures if a conflict is not resolved. Signatories of the memorandum of understanding are limited to those signatories of the LOS Treaty eligible for PIP. Effectively the main participants in the Canadian process now are Canada, the USSR, Japan (although not a signatory), India, and possibly a few other developed countries. However, such a memorandum of understanding is not capable of correcting the defects in the PIP resolution.

Conclusion

Most seabed mining countries have concluded that the UNCLOS III regime is an unsatisfactory vehicle for making major investments. None has come forward with a ringing endorsement of the seabed mining regime in the LOS Treaty. Although some feel that the Preparatory Commission may produce results sufficient to make access to minerals less arbitrary, in the U.S. view this is virtually impossible because the Authority's fundamentally flawed institutional structure cannot be repaired. The Reagan administration, therefore, will continue to press ahead toward the conclusion of other arrangements for the mutual recognition of seabed mining licenses granted by national authorities pursuant to their domestic legislation.

IV

Law of the Sea and the Future of International Order

8

JOSEPH S. NYE, JR.

Political Lessons of the New Law of the Sea Regime

The new Reagan administration faced a dilemma. Should it accept or reject an international draft treaty for the governance of the oceans over which the United States had negotiated for more than a decade? The draft treaty was far from perfect, but abandoning the process at such a late stage could also be costly. Still, the administration chose rejection.

The dilemma might have been eased if we had successfully negotiated the additional concessions we had sought.[1] For a variety of reasons, some internal to the administration, this proved impossible.[2] But even if renegotiation had succeeded, our experience with the Law of the Sea Conference raises a number of larger questions about America's ability to influence the formulation of international regimes to govern increasingly complex international interdependence.

The traditional regime that governed ocean space and resources was "freedom of the seas." The high seas belonged to no one and coastal state jurisdiction was restricted within narrow limits. Customary law was enforced by the great naval powers, particularly Britain. Maritime powers, given their de facto superiority over ocean space, had a national interest in a regime that maximized that space. At the same time, so long as the technology of navigation, fishing, and resource exploitation was limited, a regime that treated the oceans as a commons open to all was beneficial to smaller states as well.

During the first quarter century after World War II, the overall regime was not fundamentally challenged, but there were serious signs of erosion. As a result, the major maritime powers, particularly the United States and Great Britain, led efforts to reform, codify, and protect shelf and fishery jurisdiction in 1945 that unlocked Pandora's Box. While the United States tried to argue that these were separate issues, the Latin American states were provoked to claim broader territorial seas.

The last decade and a half has been marked by a widening challenge to the fundamental principles of the classical free-seas regime. Of the 150 or so states in the Third United Nations Conference on the Law of the Sea (UNCLOS III), only a minority were adherents to the 1958 Geneva Conventions. The issue of deep seabed resources and the technological developments in offshore drilling and tanker construction have raised concerns about the middle and bottom of the oceans, which were not major problems before. Less-developed countries, fearing that the commons will be exploited solely by the technologically advanced under a laissez-faire regime, have stressed broad extension of national jurisdiction and/or the need for a strong international regulatory body. Countries like Canada and Australia, once closely allied with maritime powers on ocean questions during the Cold War era, switched to a more coastal view of their interests. And even in the United States and Great Britain, important groups like oil companies and coastal fisheries led these naval powers to assert 200-mile jurisdiction over resources.

In 1960, only a quarter of all coastal states claimed jurisdiction to 12 miles or beyond. By the beginning of UNCLOS III in 1973, more than half claimed such jurisdiction. And as important as the extension of jurisdiction was the challenge to the basic principle of freedom of the seas. The last decade has been not merely one of nibbling away the margins of the regime, but also one of pressure for an alternative regime. The principle of *res nullius*, the legal doctrine that a thing without an owner belongs to the first finder, has been challenged. The new LOS Treaty basically fences off more than a third of the resources in the global oceans commons. Moreover, the mineral resources remaining outside these extended national jurisdictions have been declared to be commonly owned by all nations rather than free for the taking by any nation.

Increasing Complexity

There have also been important changes in the complexity and linkage of the various aspects of the ocean policy issues. From the perspective of U.S. foreign policy, coastal fisheries and infringement of navigation to enforce antismuggling measures were the issues in the period before 1945. Since then, new issues have included continental shelf resources, distant water fisheries, breadth of the territorial sea, deep seabed resources, arms control, freedom of scientific research, pollution, and restrictions on navigation. Moreover, the issues have become more tightly linked.

At first the great naval powers, the United States and the Soviet Union, tried to keep the seabed issue separate from other issues. In 1969, both the United States and the USSR voted against the General Assembly resolution calling for a new Law of the Sea Conference. Not until November 1970 did the United States abandon its strategy of trying to separate the territorial sea issue from the seabed issue. The U.S. Navy and the Defense Department preferred linkage because it appeared to permit trading other issues for assurances of free access for military forces.

A further aspect of the increased complexity of oceans politics has been the dramatic increase in the number of actors involved. In 1945, the United States consulted 4 other states about its shelf and fishery proclamations and 7 additional states about its coastal fisheries policy. In 1958, 86 states attended the first Geneva Conference. By the time of the Caracas Conference in 1973, 149 invitations were issued and 137 states actually participated. The major maritime states remained important, but the fragmentation of the Western bloc and the importance of bloc leaders in Africa, Latin America, Asia, and the landlocked countries increased the number of influential states to a score or more.

Our changing oceans policy agenda reflects this growth in the number of actors and of linkages among subissues. In 1945, U.S. government actions in response to anticipated offshore drilling and pressures by coastal fishermen initially set the agenda. Subsequently, Latin American and other extensions of jurisdiction set our agenda. Today, much of the agenda results from the efforts of less-developed and coastal states to control fishing, to benefit from private offshore drilling, to control pollution caused by the shipping of oil, and to prevent, regulate, or benefit from transnational scientific research. Other issues, like the debate on seabed resources, arose primarily from UN conference diplomacy. The contrast with British naval hegemony in the 19th century—the simple days of fish and ships—could not be more striking.

Unilateral and International Interests

Given the political events leading to the LOS Conference, it is not surprising that Americans were divided about the draft treaty that it produced. Some felt that it would be unwise to sign the treaty because the outcome of the process was so distant from the American view of the world. On the other hand, the treaty could come into force upon ratification by 60 states—only half of the less-developed countries involved in the process. By refusing to accede, the U.S. could find itself in an awkward legal position, caught between two conflicting regimes: one old, supported by a few strong states, and one new, supported by the many.

At the beginning of the last decade, the U.S. defined its security interests in terms of free passage through straits and access to as much water as possible for its naval forces. From this point of view, the great danger was creeping jurisdiction by coastal states. It was feared that extensions of jurisdiction to cover natural resources would take the form of extended territorial seas that would interfere with our naval forces. The extension of territorial seas to even 12-mile limits would close more than 100 straits of possible interest to the navy. Thus it was worth trying to bargain away certain aspects of the resources regime to insure freedom of the seas for our naval forces. This perception led the U.S. to agree to the comprehensive approach of a large conference.

The critics of the treaty recognized the importance of naval forces, including the ability of our navy to project force overseas and to pass freely through straits. They argued that there were better alternatives for protecting passage through straits than signing an inadequate law of the sea treaty. In their view, the U.S. could take its stand on traditional international law and reinforce that with bilateral diplomacy in the cases of the few straits that really mattered to us. In certain instances, it might be necessary to use force for those passages that might be contended, but a few discreet uses of force might be less costly in terms of establishing our basic security interests than either acceding to unacceptable interference with navigation or paying an excessive price to attempt to protect navigation by treaty.

The major concern of most critics was with the seabed mining regime. In practical economic terms, the critics argued that the key to seabed mining was to provide assured access, security of tenure, and assurance of fair and commercial terms that could make billion-and-a-half dollar per mine site investments feasible. The American interest was in a minimal framework needed to assure orderly international seabed mining. On the other hand, from the start the Group of 77 wanted a unitary international system in which the international community would both own and manage seabed mining. In 1976, then Secretary of State Henry Kissinger suggested a compromise that would split the difference between the two antithetical views by establishing a "parallel system." Private and state companies would be licensed to mine on one "side" of the system, while the other side would consist of minesites to be managed by an international authority. The Group of 77 pressed further for what it called "effective parallel systems." This meant that technology would have to be transferred and finances provided to make sure that the international authority would be ready and able to control the seabed mining system. In addition, land-based producers of the minerals that would be derived from the seabed insisted upon production limits on the seabed mining to protect them against any reduction of

their potential economic rents from mining. Secretary Kissinger
agreed to these additional demands—subject to the provision that
the negotiated regime would assure U.S. access to the mineral
resources on commercial terms.

The critics of the treaty argued that it did not assure that access, and they suggested further that the prospects for seabed
mining were not so good that we could afford to sign an inadequate
treaty. Defenders argued that the parallel system under the overall supervision of the International Seabed Authority (in which we
would have some degree of control through weighted voting) provided sufficient grounds for international seabed mining.

The critics also objected to the seabed mining provisions in
terms of the precedents they set. In their view, many of the less-
developed countries were interested in establishing a unitary international management system in order to lay the groundwork
for a fundamental redistribution of global power. Defenders of the
treaty disputed the significance of this criticism. They claimed
that more immediate vital interests of the United States in a comprehensive law of the sea outweighed the disadvantages of possible bad precedents in part of the treaty. Free transit through
straits and access of naval ships in other nations' exclusive economic zones deserved priority, they contended, noting that half
the world trade in oil passed through the Straits of Hormuz and
that American naval forces in the Indian Ocean became increasingly important after the Iranian revolution and the Soviet
occupation of Afghanistan. Treaty defenders asserted that instead
of the proposed free-transit regime, customary international law
might have evolved toward a 300-mile territorial sea had there not
been negotiations in which free transit could be secured in return
for compromises on seabed issues. They claimed that unilateral
naval initiatives would become more costly simply in military
terms as more and more countries acquired military technology—
notably patrol boats, land-based aircraft, and antiship missiles—
that could give them effective control over extended territorial jurisdictions. Furthermore, they argued, it was unlikely that we
would be able to maintain a consistent unilateral policy and program to enforce our jurisdictional claims; each of our embassies
would constantly press for exceptions and the preservation of cor-
dial bilateral relations.

Defenders admitted that many provisions of the convention were inconvenient though necessary compromises. As Elliot Richardson put it,

the changes in customary international law that have gained the most momentum from consensus in the Law of the Seas Conference are those that enlarge coastal state claims. While these expansive principles may not need the treaty's entry into force in order to be ultimately absorbed into customary international law, the same cannot be so confidently said of the limitation and qualification on coastal states' rights that the treaty would attach to them. The provisions for transit passage through straits qualify the extension of the territorial sea; the provisions for sea lanes through archipelagoes limit the concept of the Archipelagic waters; the provisions preserving high seas freedom in the exclusive economic zone restrain coastal state claims of control; the provisions for geographic limits bar claims beyond those limits. These provisions can spell the difference between enjoying and losing high seas freedom of navigation, overflight, and related uses in 40 percent of the world's oceans.

In short, wrote Richardson, "any treaty that can win widespread acceptance is bound to have costs as well as benefits. . . . Its measure is whether it serves all our interests as well as or better than those interests would be served in a treatyless world."[3]

American Power and Regime Change

Does it matter when the United States turns its back on a major ten-year effort at international regime definition? Some answer no, arguing that a great power has the alternative of military force to defend its interests. But we cannot understand the outcome of the law of the sea negotiations unless we understand the changes that have occurred in the role of force as an instrument of power in today's more complex world politics. Traditionalists find it anomalous that the greatest naval power in the postwar world was unable to impose its will upon its allies in an area where it was allegedly a regional hegemony—i.e., Latin America—or that Britain would lose a "cod war" with a weak state like Iceland.

Naval force played a role in the politics of rule-making in the oceans in the postwar period, but only after passing through the distorting prism of international organizations. Prescriptions that urge returning solely to the use of force fail to understand the broader changes that have made those international organizations a significant part of international politics. The multiplicity of goals of the superpowers and the multiple channels of modern communications and transportation, as well as the increased costliness of the use of force, help explain why the alternatives to the current law of the sea outcomes were more limited than some of the critics admit.

The increased complexity of world politics has reduced the potential for any country to exercise control over the whole system. There are more states and more issues and less hierarchy in international politics. For example, there are three times as many states in the United Nations today as at the time of its founding in 1945. Moreover, our foreign policy agenda has become more complex. Added to the classic issues of military security and international trade are issues such as food, population, environmental destruction, the governance of space, climate modification, terrorism, and a whole host of others.

Furthermore, the role of military force in world politics has changed. In general, force has become more costly for great powers, particularly democratic ones, to apply effectively in world politics. This is an issue that is frequently misunderstood. While it was fashionable in the aftermath of Vietnam to argue that force had lost its effectiveness, that was clearly not the case, then or now. Force remains the most effective form of power in many issues and in many situations. But it often proves to be the most *costly* form of power. Indeed, in some circumstances the use of force costs more than its goals are worth. The military balance of power remains the bedrock or necessary condition of a sound foreign policy, but it is difficult to apply to many of the interdependence issues on our foreign policy agenda.

The use of force is made more costly for major states by four conditions: risk of nuclear escalation, uncertain and possibly negative effects on the achievement of other goals, resistance by socially aroused nationalistic populations in otherwise weak states, and domestic concern in democracies about the moral cost of the use of force. Even states relatively unaffected by the fourth condition, such as the Communist countries, feel some constraints from the first three. For example, the Soviet invasion of Afghanistan and the threat of invasion of Poland may prove effective, but they may also prove more costly in terms of the second and third conditions than was true in the past. On the other hand, given modern technologies, terrorist groups and lesser states involved in regional rivalries may find it *easier* to use force. The net effect of these changes in the role of force is to erode somewhat the international hierarchy traditionally based upon military power.

This erosion of international hierarchy is sometimes portrayed as a decline of American power, as though the causes lay entirely in our internal processes. Admittedly, from the perspective of a policymaker of the 1950s there has been some decline, but American power in the sense of resources has not declined as dramatically as is often supposed. Representing nearly one quarter of world military expenditure and world economic product, the U.S. is still the most powerful state in the world.

To understand what has changed in the world, one must distinguish power over others from power over outcomes. What the U.S. is experiencing is not so much an erosion of power resources or leverage as exercised against any single country (although there has been some) but an erosion of our power to control outcomes in the international system as a whole. The main reason is that this system itself has become more complex with the addition of more issues and more actors, and with the decline of hierarchy. We are less well placed to extract unilaterally the positions that we prefer. Multilateral diplomacy and international institutions have become more important because so much of the agenda is concerned with organizing collective actions. While increased military budgets can help to remedy some aspects of our current international position, we cannot hope simply to spend ourselves out of the increasing complexity of world politics.

One must be careful, of course, not to overstate the degree of change in world politics. In a world of sovereign states, military force and the balance of power will always be a necessary condition for stability. But interdependence is also an important source of power in the international system. As long as analysts insist on a false dichotomy between realism and economic interdependence, policy prescriptions will oscillate between an over- and an under-reliance on the role of force, when they should be integrating force with other policy instruments into an effective strategy. In particular, we are likely to underinvest in the creation and maintenance of the international regimes that govern interdependence.[4]

As a great power, the United States has an interest in an established world order and in maintaining the generally accepted rules, norms, or procedures that govern the interactions in a given issue. We live in a world of these international regimes. Regimes vary greatly in terms of scope, area, and membership, and their sheer number is striking. They deal with everything from monetary issues to international trade, from management of natural resources to the management of particular geographical areas, from the conservation of species to the control of armaments.

Traditionally, great powers interested in world order have had the greatest interest in the formation and maintenance of international regimes, and the regimes tended to reflect the dictates of the great powers. The strong nations made the rules. This presents us with a basic dilemma in current world politics.

The United States is the leading state in an era in which there can only be leadership without hegemony. As a great power we can still take unilateral initiatives, particularly if they are designed to help move others in the direction of multiple leadership. Leadership by example will often be important. But overall, there will have to be a higher degree of coordination of our position with those of other states than was true for Britain in the nineteenth century or for the United States in the extraordinary period immediately following the end of World War II.

International Regimes and National Objectives

What do we do, then, when we are faced with a multilateral process that we cannot fully control, that produces regime change that we find flawed? One place to start is to learn from our experience with the Law of the Sea Conference to draw some general conclusions about U.S. foreign policy and international regimes.

Because the United States is a great power with a general interest in world order, the building and maintenance of international regimes tend to be in our national interest. Orderly processes allow us to pursue the multiplicity of our interests in a manner that reduces their mutual interference and the costs of trade-offs. The existence of international regimes allows for greater moderation in foreign policy and reduces the degree of the constant risks that statesmen encounter.

It does not follow, however, that all international regimes are in our interest. For example, efforts in UNESCO to negotiate a "New World Information Order" could seriously interfere with journalists' access to news. Many aspects of the "New International Economic Order" stressed in the rhetoric of UN forums would not serve our interests (nor the economic interests of many poor countries). It may be that the absence of a regime has made oil imports more unpredictable and increased our insecurity, but it does not follow that the kind of regime we might recreate in global negotiations would really reduce our uncertainty and insecurity. On the contrary, a bad regime might well increase them.[5]

Even if we decide that creating or revising a regime is in our national interest, it does not follow that entering into broad-based conference negotiations is the best way to pursue that interest. In fact, conference diplomacy is only one among a number of instruments that can be used in the process of regime formulation. While it might seem paradoxical at first, unilateral action can play an important role in regime construction. Indeed, traditionally the unilateral actions of great powers were major sources of regime formulation. As we have seen, this is less the case under current political conditions, but there is still a role for these actions. Leadership often requires someone to go first. The crucial points are that the unilateral actions should retain some inducement for others to follow, and that the actions should be consistent with our long-term regime goals. In the oceans area, Truman's proclamations in 1945 failed to meet these criteria. Similarly, our 1976 fisheries legislation did not help regime leadership, because we were eroding constraints before the negotiations were over. On the other hand, carefully formulated interim legislation to encourage the beginning of seabed mining probably helped to move the LOS negotiations forward.

A special form of unilateral instrument is the use of military force. Judiciously used (or threatened) military force can play a critical role in regime formulation. The knowledge that great powers could and would, at least in principle, assert and defend their naval rights of passage through contested waters certainly played a useful background role in the bargaining at the LOS Conference. On the other hand, indiscriminate use of force can prove too costly in relation to the particular interests sought. Shooting our way through straits can poison bilateral relations with states whose cooperation we need in other issues on our complex foreign policy agenda. Moreover, the use of force may generate resentment that can interfere with broader alliance relationships or with negotiations for regime formulation. A key consideration, then, is the coupling of force with legitimacy. If military actions are broadly regarded as justifiable, at home and abroad, the cost of the military instrument can be reduced. Above all, it is critical that unilateral actions, including the use of force, be considered in relation to our overall goals for a regime and to their impact on our bilateral or multilateral negotiations before they are attempted.

Thus the United States must see a real prospect that negotiations will lead to a satisfactory regime and improved conditions for our interests before we embark upon complex and lengthy conferences. We need to ask ourselves at least three questions before starting.

First, what is the nature of the issue? If it clearly involves collective or indivisible goods, how many key actors must be involved to create or preserve an effective regime? The same questions can be asked about divisible goods, with the possibility that the key players can be more limited. Given the concentration of technology and capabilities in space, for example, as contrasted with the oceans, there is less incentive to pay the costs of multilateral conference diplomacy.

Second, even if we decide that the nature of the issue requires broad participation, we must ask if the time is ripe for fruitful conference diplomacy. Will our ability to promote and protect our interests improve or erode with time? Would the beginning of negotiations foreclose some desirable options and open a Pandora's Box of unmanageable issues? Would failed negotiations make existing difficulties significantly worse? One would have expected, a priori, that the geographically disadvantaged states would rally to the U.S. trusteeship and revenue-sharing proposals of 1970. But they did not. Instead they were recruited via bloc and regional politics into Group of 77 positions largely established by Latin American coastal states that had a ten-year lead in thinking about the issues. By the time the landlocked and geographically disadvantaged states had learned enough to begin to carefully differentiate their interests, it was largely too late. From the U.S.

point of view, we got too far into conference diplomacy before the time was ripe to build the coalitions we needed.

The third question we must ask before embarking on complex multilateral diplomacy relates to domestic politics. Can we ratify the results? Are the domestic and congressional perceptions so at odds with what is negotiable internationally that the process will be greeted by a Senate rejection? If so, we may be worse off than not to have entered the process at all, and should refrain from doing so until opinion on the issue at home and abroad has progressed further.

U.S. Preparation for Future Negotiations

Perhaps the most important lesson from our experience with the Third Law of the Sea Conference is that we need to prepare ourselves much better before we enter multilateral negotiations.

Before agreeing to participate in a conference, we must insist on adequate international preparations. Ideally, a suitable small body should work on texts for submission. Even when this is the case, we must pay closer attention to the effect of bloc politics on the appointment of chairmen and drafting officers. Identifying in advance an able president and reasonable chairmen and then firmly refusing to agree to others will be crucial. Much of the difference in the progress between the First and Second Committees in the LOS Conference was attributable to the difference in chairmen. The agenda is also important. The packaging of issues in committees and the order of their treatment can strongly affect outcomes.

In the substantive negotiations, we have to be cautious about making large dramatic compromises in principle and then finding that the rigidity of the Group of 77 means that we have given up a principle for nothing. We must be aware of the slippery slope effect before we decide to alter our positions, whether it be to allow linkage of issues or to suggest general approaches to a solution.

We need better preparation domestically as well as internationally. Given protracted negotiations, it is essential that we plan in decade-long terms and try to identify the evolution of our interests, other countries' positions, and possible key branch points before we enter a conference. While such planning can never hope for perfect prescience, both the State Department and the National Security Council can do better than they have hitherto. It is critical to bring key trade-offs to high-level attention before the real options have been traded away. Given the size and unwieldiness of our delegations (which in turn reflect the diversity of our interests), early clarification of high-level instructions is doubly important.

We also need to consider how to relate our domestic and foreign interests on issues that have a leg in each domain. In today's transnational systems, our domestic policy actions can complement or undercut our international actions. Certainly, failure to think through the way our domestic and international actions affect each other can create a countervailing rather than reinforcing effect.

In the 1950s, when Latin American states were arresting our tuna fishermen, we took the pressure out of the transnational system by passing the Fisherman's Protective Act, by which our Treasury reimbursed the fishermen for their fines. But it also meant that we "blinked" in the confrontation over principle. However, on the question of launching seabed mining, some forms of domestic insurance for the early stages of investment against the subsequent prospect of international red tape's halting mining could make sense both domestically and internationally.

Finally, on the domestic side, we must further develop our procedures of congressional involvement in negotiations to protect against later failures to ratify. The LOS advisory process seems to have worked reasonably well. There may be further lessons to be learned from the successful case of the Multilateral Trade Negotiations.

Whatever one thinks of the outcome, we need to learn from our experiences with the Law of the Sea Conference. We should not repeat our performance in other conferences. Over the coming decades, the U.S. will remain a dominant power in world politics, but the complexity of world politics will continue to increase. As a great power with diverse interests we will have a strong national interest in the creation and maintenance of satisfactory international regimes. A far-sighted definition of our interest in international regimes will be critical to our success in world politics. It is time that we paid more careful attention to how to pursue that interest.

9

BERNARD H. OXMAN

The Two Conferences

It often seems that American proponents and opponents of the new convention on the law of the sea are talking about two different documents. Yet with respect to the treaty's subject matter, its organization, and even in some ways its objectives, the different readings are not necessarily contradictory. Rather, they reflect different ideas of public and private rights, of the meaning of international law, and of the role of the United States as an industrial, capitalist, coastal, and maritime state in the world community.

The treaty's partisans emphasize its provisions dealing with the traditional problem of the law of the sea—the resolution of the tension between coastal state jurisdiction over adjacent waters and the freedoms of the seas—and the newer manifestations of this problem, including jurisdiction to protect and preserve the marine environment and the role of compulsory third-party dispute settlement. They find the convention desirable because it promises to produce greater order, stability, and predictability; to protect free navigation and military uses; and to minimize international friction.

The adversaries of the treaty are troubled by its provisions governing seabed mining beyond coastal state jurisdiction. They argue that the convention overly restricts the actions of states and individuals, and they decry what they see as invidious collectivist restraints on initiative.

The relationship between restraint and freedom of action lies at the heart of the matter. It is presumably common ground that it is often desirable to restrain claims of other states to *control* use of the sea in order to promote our freedom to *use* the sea.

Different Desires for a New Convention

In terms of the traditional uses of the sea, particularly navigation, the threat to freedom of use came from the accelerating claims of coastal states to control the use of the sea in ever broader areas off their coasts. In order to preserve their flexibility to use the seas to the maximum extent, particularly for navigation and military purposes, the United States, the Soviet Union, and their maritime allies began planning a law of the sea conference in 1966 and 1967 for the purpose of halting this trend by fixing a narrow maximum permissible breadth of the territorial sea of coastal states, guaranteeing freedom of transit through straits covered by such territorial seas, and entrenching navigational and military freedoms seaward of the territorial sea. Complementing these maritime objectives (but not necessarily inconsistent with them) was the drive of many coastal states to secure control over fisheries and seabed minerals for great distances off their coasts.

On an entirely separate track at the time, Ambassador Arvid Pardo of Malta called in 1967 for an international system to regulate the seabeds beyond the limits of coastal state jurisdiction. Like the maritime powers, he hoped to contain the expanding claims of coastal states to control the uses of the sea. Unlike the maritime powers, he also sought to regulate claims of freedom to use the seabeds.

The maritime powers and some others saw a treaty as helpful to their efforts to prevent further restraint on navigational and military freedoms; the coastal states saw it as helpful to their efforts to restrain freedom of action with respect to huge coastal resources; and Ambassador Pardo and those he inspired saw it as an effort to control the expansion of both coastal state restraints and freedom of action with respect to deep seabed resources. Most states fell into at least two of these groups noted above. No two had identical conceptions of the proper balance between restraint and freedom on all issues.

The merger of the maritime and coastal states' objectives with the objectives of Ambassador Pardo and his followers in a single comprehensive conference on the law of the sea is better described as platonic cohabitation than marriage. The question of deep seabed mining was put into one committee of the whole. All of the traditional law of the sea issues were put into another. (For reasons of geographic balance in the distribution of chairman-ships, a third committee was created to deal with pollution and scientific research.) Throughout most of the conference, delegation heads concentrated on the traditional maritime issues in the Second Committee. Delegates dealing with deep seabed mining in the First Committee tended to be younger, more aggressive, and often less constrained by precisely defined national interests, governmental instructions, or political reputations.

Problems in the American Debate

It is also notable that some proponents of the treaty tend to speak more often of "interests," while some opponents tend to speak more often of "principles." This is not to suggest that the former's "interests" are unprincipled or that the latter's "principles" are disinterested. But it may suggest that the tendency of the treaty draftsmen to resort to ambiguity, obfuscation and, in particular, hyperbole may evoke less sympathy in the latter group.

This being said, it is necessary for the serious student of this subject to note that two characteristics of the decade-long debate regarding the conference and the convention on the law of the sea are both an astonishing lack of familiarity with the text as a whole by some commentators and a passionate preconceived commitment to preordained conclusions by others. The object (although not necessarily the subject) of the debate is international law—more particularly, the rules of international law applicable at sea.

Every analysis must, in the end, be based upon an appraisal of the realistic alternatives in that context. A confusion of law with legal argument by some commentators and an ignorance of international law by others raise doubts about the nature and extent of rational dialogue in the American debate.

It is of more than incidental interest that the domestic debate over the Law of the Sea Convention may be a skirmish in the larger campaign of economists and their disciples (including some lawyers) to wrest control of the processes of governmental policy from the "legal establishment." While it is natural that the revolutionary arguments of the economists might appeal to those who feel that they have been disfranchised by that establishment—in this case, some conservatives—the same theme is echoed by a Carter administration economist. Yielding to the Clemenceau temptation, he believes that the law of the sea—and presumably most of the rest of international law—is too important to be left to the lawyers. In this connection, it might be noted that a number of the treaty compromises regarding deep seabed mining that economic and political science theorists find particularly offensive were formulated in principle not by lawyers but by an eminent political scientist, then serving as secretary of state, with the advice of a former president and chairman of the board of the most successful high-technology corporation in the world, who was then serving as the president's special representative for the law of the sea.

Nevertheless, the remark about lawyers is certainly true in at least one respect. The question concerns "title" to deep seabed mining sites.

Property Rights and Confused Discourse

One of the things that distinguishes a property right from other rights is its exclusive character—a right to exclude all others. Therefore, the right must in principle be valid against all of the rest of the world.

The more one asserts that an activity is of great significance, but cannot be conducted without a clear property right, the more one reminds the public—in its manifestation either as a national legislature or as a diplomatic conference of states—that it may have something of value to sell. One should not be surprised if the public draws the appropriate conclusion. What the public is selling in fact is its acquiescence in, and cooperation in enforcing, legitimated exclusivity. It is for essentially formal or rhetorical reasons that a fiction of public "property" is invented to give substance to the sale, be it the notion that radio waves are public property or that the deep seabeds are the common heritage of mankind.

Senior lawyers and economists of the State Department and Treasury Department, Republican and Democrat alike, were often skeptical of the insistence on the need for clear property rights in order to skim vast areas of the seabed for manganese nodules. It was some mining companies, and more particularly some lawyers they hired for this issue only, who insisted—in the context of negotiations with the rest of the world—that they must have "clear" property rights in writing as against the rest of the world in order to obtain financing. Ironically, many of the very same companies and lawyers now say that their needs can be fully met if their minesites are respected by the nationals of a minority of industrial states under a reciprocal arrangement.

A basic error of analysis contributed to this problem, an error for which lawyers and economists share responsibility. It involves the assimilation of private rights and governmental rights, of private law and public law, ultimately of property and sovereignty. While there is no doubt that the promotion of the private interests of citizens is a primary motivating factor, most lawmaking negotiations among states, when conservatively conceived, have concerned the allocation of public powers among states and their obligations to each other in the exercise of those powers. Private property rights derive from the exercise of allocated powers by a state; they are not a direct object of such intergovernmental negotiations.

Public international law is primarily concerned with the maintenance of the prerequisites for all fruitful human activity, including economic activity: the promotion of peace, public order, and reasonable stability of expectations among separate societies organized in accordance with different values. Its purpose is not to promote homogeneity of political, economic, social, or cultural values or practices. It assumes the existence of diversity (and associated suspicions) and exists to maintain reasonable order within that diversity.

The purpose of allocating public powers among states by treaty is to reduce conflict among them. This is done by narrowing the situations in which conflicting assertions of power may occur and by channeling those that do occur into more manageable legal and technical contexts.

If the reason for allocating rights is to promote peace, public order, and reasonable stability of expectations within the context of a diversity of values and systems, then we must define what we mean by rights in light of those goals. It will not do to speak of God-given rights that may be contested by others, perhaps even violently. However divine the source for the assertion of rights, however eminent the authorities defending that assertion, however just or appealing the purported ends, if the assertion is not accepted by others then there are no rights in the functional sense that we mean here: namely, the acquiescence by others in the legitimacy of the activity in question.

The key words here are "others" and "acquiescence." Which "others" do we mean? Given the underlying purpose of achieving the acquiescence, by "others" we mean those states in a position to disrupt the desired stability of expectations by military, economic, or political means. By "acquiescence" we mean a decision to accept the assertion of a right without military, economic, or political challenge, even though the state in question might prefer that the underlying right in question not exist or that its specific exercise be avoided.

Like much of the rest of modern international law, the international law of the sea evolved largely in unwritten form as "customary international law," a term used by international lawyers to distinguish it from international law in written treaty form. The traditional evidence of customary international law is the custom and practice of states.

There is nothing unusual about relying on unwritten rules. Most of the norms of behavior that guide us in our everyday lives— whether or not we call them law—are unwritten in form. Most of the promises that we make to each other in the course of our everyday lives are unwritten.

One difficulty with unwritten rules is that as the composition of the community or the scope of the problems involved increases in variety or complexity, the demands for definitive and authoritative statements of the rules increase. This written law can take the form of judicial decisions interpreting what the customary law (or vaguely worded written law) is, assuming those judicial decisions are in fact accepted as having legislative effect as precedent. It can also take the form of direct written statements of the governing principles as national legislation or international lawmaking treaties.

Clarification of International Law

At the present stage, resort to the International Court of Justice or other tribunals for the resolution of disputes between states is relatively rare. Moreover, judicial decisions are not formally accepted as authoritative statements of international law in the sense that the decisions of American courts on common law issues are regarded as binding precedent. Thus in the twentieth century the so-called lawmaking treaty has increasingly been resorted to as a way of building greater stability of expectations (that is, of "building" international law) in an expanded community of states faced with more complex interactions.

The historical function of the conference called to negotiate a lawmaking treaty is to increase the efficiency and certainty of the lawmaking and law-finding processes. It is like a switchboard. The conference brings together all of those "others" described in order to reach a common decision on what they will acquiesce in.

The question of which states form the relevant group depends upon the issue. If one is speaking about transit of straits, for example, it seems that the relevant group would consist primarily of the states along major straits and of the major users of the straits. Presumably each of the states would because of its underlying interest have the will, and because of its underlying position have the ability, to upset the stability of expectations regarding transit of straits of it chose to do so. Similarly, if the written law embodied in a treaty is to create rights in the sense that we mean them here—that is, to enhance peace, public order, and stability of expectations—then these states must by and large also accept the resulting rules.

A multilateral conference like the Third United Nations Conference on the Law of the Sea assembles all of the states of the world to discuss all of the major issues and allocation of rights regarding ocean uses. This permits groups with relatively greater determination and importance—like the maritime powers in the case of straits—to generate broad support on issues that do not strongly engage the majority. But it also creates a temptation to regard the assembled participants as representatives of all mankind dispatched to enunciate global community policy on its behalf, rather than as instructed negotiating agents of states. The result is a rhetorical pressure to cast issues in terms of community values (and especially in terms of the interests of the numerical majority) to a degree that far exceeds the actual weight accorded such considerations by national governments in their individual formulations of foreign policy.

Such pressure can have beneficial effects. For example, in controlling the spread of pollution or disease, it exposes both the necessity for and the possibility of effective action on a global level. But the rhetorical pressure to submerge national interests in the face of asserted community objectives can also greatly magnify the influence of those who have little at stake in the resolution of a particular issue and who would not be in a strong position to affect the underlying stability of expectations outside the context of a multilateral conference. Up to a point, this too can be useful, since it assures that more voices are heard and may enhance support for the outcome. But if it diverts a conference from its primary function of serving as a forum for working out more efficiently the norms acceptable to those who are principally affected, then the resulting document will not define rights in the sense we are using the term here.

Postwar Developments and the Need for New Law

Against this background, one may examine the major development in the law of the sea since World War II. That development entails the removal of most of the living resources of the sea and most of the known oil and gas resources of the seabed from the high seas regime—from the "commons" as it were—and their allocation to the adjacent coastal states. This process was begun in 1945 when the United States claimed exclusive control over the resources of the seabed of the continental shelf adjacent to its coast and outside its 3-mile territorial sea. It was continued as Latin American countries, and then others, claimed various types of jurisdiction over the waters as well as the seabed in 200-mile zones adjacent to their coasts.

In 1958, the first United Nations Conference on the Law of the Sea confirmed this trend with respect to seabed resources of the continental shelf, but was vague as to precisely how much of the seabed was involved in the allocation of resources to the coastal states. That conference took a conservative approach to the question of extending coastal state rights over living resources in the water column. Thus, sufficient precision was lacking with respect to the outer limit of coastal state control over seabed resources, a question that became increasingly relevant to stability of expectations as interest emerged in developing seabed resources in deeper areas further from shore. Secondly, the approach to fisheries resources taken at the 1958 conference did not respond to the growing demands of coastal states for control over fisheries in vast areas adjacent to their coasts. This was one of the principal reasons why the 1958 conventions never achieved universal ratification.

By contrast, the Third United Nations Conference on the Law of the Sea—functioning by consensus—developed texts that fully reflect and refine the trend toward allocating most marine fisheries and hydrocarbon resources to adjacent coastal states. While establishing a maximum permissible breadth of 12 nautical miles for the territorial sea, the new convention on the law of the sea achieves this reallocation by the use of two regimes seaward of the territorial sea: the continental shelf and the exclusive economic zone.

The conference confirmed the preexisting continental shelf regime, which allows the coastal state to exercise exclusive sovereign rights over the exploration and exploitation of the natural resources of the seabed and subsoil of the continental shelf. What the convention adds is a broad and more precise outer limit designed to place virtually all known hydrocarbon potential under coastal state jurisdiction.*

The convention mandates the establishment of minimum international environmental standards for the development of the

---

*See Appendix for a more complete description.

resources of the continental shelf that coastal states would have to observe, assuming they did not wish to establish higher standards for such activities. While the environmental reasons for taking such a step are clear, economic reasons were also involved:

- Pollution resulting from oil or gas drilling off the coast of one country may be widely publicized, thereby increasing public resistance to the development of oil and gas resources off the coasts of other countries.

- Pollution resulting from oil drilling off the coast of one country can be carried by winds and currents to other areas, thereby damaging the economic interests of another country in tourism, recreation, and fishing.

- Offshore oil drilling is a global industry that can achieve certain economies as a result of standardization of requirements regarding design and construction of equipment and certain on-site operations.

About 90 percent of the world's fishing takes place within 200 miles of the coast of some country. Therefore, the effect of the establishment of a 200-mile economic zone is to replace the previous regime of freedom of fishing on the high seas by a regime of coastal state control. The convention introduces three new elements in this regime for fisheries:

- It contains special provisions regarding the management of migrating fish stocks that pay no heed to the allocative boundaries drawn by man—in some cases differentiating among species of fish.

- It requires states to establish conservation measures for fish stocks, including the establishment of an allowable catch, with a view to maintaining an optimum yield from fish stocks over time.

- It requires coastal states to ensure the "optimum utilization" of fish stocks in their zone. If the fishermen of the coastal state are not for the time being able to take the full allowable catch of particular stocks, the state must allow foreign fishermen access to those stocks under reasonable terms and conditions.

The "duty of optimum utilization" is a particularly interesting innovation from the perspective of food and resource policy. In effect, it prohibits substantial underutilization of a renewable resource so long as there is a market for it. The duty is a response to the recognition that there are a variety of political pressures on coastal states not to permit foreign exploitation of fisheries resources off their coasts even though they gain little if anything by allowing those resources to remain unexploited. The duty of optimum utilization was intended to reduce this political restraint on the normal operation of economic forces. While the coastal state may establish reasonable conditions for access to the resources, and while those conditions may include rent that increases the cost of extraction of the living resources in question, it may not completely prohibit their extraction (unless required for conservation). The duty of optimum utilization is therefore a response to the global interest in ensuring the maximum feasible supply of animal protein from the sea consistent with sound conservation practices, as well as to the more immediate interest of distant-water fishing states in preserving some access to fisheries resources that fall under the jurisdiction of various coastal states.

Geography and Political and Economic Interests

It is important to bear in mind that the pressure to extend coastal state control over ocean resources was not confined to poor developing countries. With respect to seabed resources, it originated in the United States. With respect to fisheries, it originated in South American countries that are not among the poorest of the developing countries. Such Western countries as Australia, Canada, Iceland, New Zealand, Norway, the United Kingdom, and the United States were among the advocates of very broad coastal state control over seabed resources or fisheries resources, or both, at the conference.

Nevertheless, the rhetorical technique used by the Latin American states to persuade their colleagues in Asia and Africa of the merits of broad coastal state jurisdiction was that such extensions of jurisdiction would benefit developing countries generally. The argument was that under a high seas regime, the exploitation of resources would be dominated by the fishing fleets and mining

companies of the developed world. Broad coastal state jurisdiction
would permit developing coastal states to:

- protect local fishermen from foreign competition;

- prohibit or restrict development of resources until there could
  be greater participation in the extraction or downsteam economic exploitation of those resources;

- collect economic rent for the privilege of exploiting such resources in the form of cash or training and technology transfer.

The effort, therefore, was a reallocation of wealth to the coastal
state that presumably would not otherwise result from the operation of market forces. Whether one believes that such forced
reallocation will ultimately prove beneficial to the world economy
depends partly on one's economic philosophy. One of the interesting things about the debate on the law of the sea is that those who
oppose artificial restraints on market development of deep seabed
resources have paid little attention to the fact that a primary mo-
tive for extending coastal state jurisdiction over the much more
valuable resources of the economic zone and the continental shelf
is precisely to impose artificial restraints.

It is of course true that extending coastal state control over
resources can make a significant contribution to the economic
development of coastal states that have major coastal fisheries or
oil resources. Accordingly, coastal state governments, even in
those countries where investment conditions are poor or unstable,
may be encouraged to supply increased incentives to economic
investment.

On the other hand, because they are either landlocked or have
small enclosed coastlines, some countries will not gain control
over significant fisheries or oil and gas resources off their coasts
from broad extensions of coastal state jurisdiction. This problem
of geography is not unique to developing countries. At the conference, a group of more than fifty landlocked and "geographically
disadvantaged" states—ranging from Lesotho to the Federal Republic of Germany—was formed in an attempt to protect their interests in the context of a massive allocation of control over
resources to coastal states.

As one might expect, in this context the rhetoric of community goals and promotion of developing countries' interests broke down. Both developing and developed coastal states asserted that there were stringent limits on the concessions they were prepared to make in a treaty to the landlocked and geographically disadvantaged states, since the coastal states could achieve many—although perhaps not all—of the advantages of the resource allocation without a treaty and without such concessions. Two concessions, however, were made:

- First, landlocked and geographically disadvantaged states enjoy a priority of access to surplus living resources of the economic zones of their coastal neighbors.

- Second, coastal states must pay a small percentage of the value of production of hydrocarbons from the continental margin in areas seaward of 200 miles into an international fund to be distributed to states parties to the law of the sea convention on the basis of equitable sharing criteria.

Community Interest and Immediate Stakes

In context, the negotiations concerning deep seabed manganese nodules were almost the obverse of those regarding the continental shelf and the exclusive economic zone. When questions of global sharing for the overall benefit of the international community were raised in connection with continental shelf or economic zone resources, the large number of coastal states seeking unfettered control over their slice of the pie resisted such appeals. With respect to deep seabed mining, however, the number of states that perceived a direct interest was quite small, and the rhetorical appeal to community interest in general, and to developing country interest in particular, severely narrowed the possibilities for accommodating immediate national interests.

This leads to a possibly unexpected conclusion that may have some bearing on approaches to other issues. The achievement of near-consensus on food, energy, and various military issues at a global conference of over 150 states functioning by consensus—while the same conference split over the issue of deep seabed manganese nodules—would seem to suggest that multilateral negotiations are more likely to succeed when the immediate national stakes are both high and fairly widely distributed.

This is not to suggest that it is either desirable or appropriate to dismiss considerations of real community interest in the development of international law. But multilateral decisions that result from careful consideration by, and dialogue among, those who are principally affected are likely to produce sound and acceptable norms of behavior. Decisions that emerge largely from the rhetorical imperatives of multilateral bodies or national ideologies are likely to produce fustian and divergent practices.

It is particularly important to recognize that the problems with the deep seabed mining regime cannot be generalized into propositions about the propriety of dealing with economic issues as a whole in multilateral forums. The most significant economic effect of the convention—the allocation to the coastal states of virtually all hydrocarbons, fish, and other marine resources likely to be exploited in this century and well into the next—satisfies many people on both sides. Developing countries that acquire jurisdiction over substantial resources off their coast see this as a redistribution of high seas wealth that would otherwise be the plunder of the mobile rich. Free-market economists argue that each coastal state will be motivated to maximize the production of wealth from its jurisdictional zones. The first group seems undeterred by the fact that a large proportion of oil and fish will be allocated to industrial and proto-industrial states with long and exposed coastlines, with none to the poorest landlocked states. The second group seems undeterred by the fact that few coastal states have offshore resource development laws that would come close to meeting free-market models for maximizing efficient development of the resources. The first group satisfied its practical economic interests, though it bent the principle of a community of less-developed states. The second group won a symbolic victory of economic principle that may yield some disappointing economic results. Thus an outcome generally acceptable to both was achieved.

Some Hypotheses

Three general hypotheses suggest themselves. At least as subjects for debate, they are probably more important than any predictions about the future of the law of the sea.

First, it is unnecessary and unwise to suppose that there is an inherent conflict between American interests and values, including those emphasized by conservatives, and the values of public international law as classically understood—namely, peace, order, and stability of expectations. It is precisely these values that lead the radical to conclude that the great political divide lies between him and both conservatives and liberals.

Second, while liberty of state action is deeply embedded in the traditions of public international law and the perceptions of governments, liberty of action of the individual, whether political or economic, unhappily is not. To the extent that freedom of action for the individual is—and for the United States, frequently will be— an underlying objective in international negotiations, it may be easier to secure that freedom of action if it is addressed on the level of public law rather than private law, namely in terms of freedom of action of states rather than of individuals or companies. The freedom of the high seas works precisely in that way. It is enjoyed by states. Liberal states like the United States then extend that freedom on more or less liberal terms to their nationals.

The problem is that each state has its own idea of the proper relation between government and citizens. Even the liberal West is divided on the question. Divergent opinions about the respective roles of governments and private investors in natural resource development are still strongly held. Each state will seek an international model for the acquisition and regulation of private rights in natural resources that approximates its own approach; different or inconsistent models are suspect. It is thus not surprising that the deep seabed mining regime reflects various contradictory understandings of the relation of private freedom and state regulations and is not entirely consistent with any one coherent view.

Third, one should be cautious about concluding that customary international law is necessarily more conducive to free enterprise than lawmaking treaties can be. Although both are imperfect, customary international law cannot offer international businessmen the same measure of precision, long-term predictability, and dispute settlement mechanisms as treaty law. These qualities may be more important to the availability of private risk capital than to government investment. In principle, an unavoidable relationship exists between risk and the extent to which there are common perceptions of legitimacy. On the other hand, it is important to consider whether the cost of a treaty, in terms of undesirable provisions, may be too high in particular circumstances.

The Future

The law of the sea is about to enter at least a decade of new struggles. The outcome is unknown.

With respect to deep seabed mining, the first question is whether the market in this century will justify the economic risks. If so, there are two further questions that miners will ask. Given a choice between the national mining laws of the United States and certain other countries and the yet-to-be-elaborated mining regulations under the Law of the Sea Convention, which system will offer a more congenial regulatory environment? To what extent will the differences in global legitimacy of the two systems affect the willingness of large banks and corporations to invest in mining ventures?

As long as the two systems remain at least potential competitors—one offering an apparently favorable regulatory environment but uncertain legitimacy, the other offering apparently widespread legitimacy but an uncertain regulatory environment—will any company make a billion-dollar investment under either system without government insurance or some other form of subsidy? A full and open debate in the United States about whether to insure or otherwise subsidize deep seabed mining is likely to bring out impressive statistics about the importance of the hard minerals involved to United States economy and security. But, particularly for those committed to the free market, such a debate is also likely to raise some difficult questions:

- How much does it serve the security or economic interests of the United States to encourage development of seabed minerals in the distant South Pacific when it could encourage further investment in mining on land in Canada (and perhaps even in the United States or its 200-mile zone)?

- What would be insured against? In particular, would the United States government insure against losses, boycotts, or other economic retaliation against unrelated activities and assets of the companies engaged in deep seabed mining and their banks?

- Is the United States government prepared to insure ventures in which there is substantial or majority foreign capital participation?

- Who will be next in line for a similar type of subsidy?

With respect to navigation, military activities, and other traditional uses of the sea, it is likely that the mere existence of the text and the rhetorical consensus on the treatment of these issues in the convention will slow the rate of change. In the short run, this likelihood will tend to confirm the views of those who believe that it is possible to stabilize the traditional law of the sea without supporting or becoming party to the convention. If past practice is a reliable guide, there is, however, reason for concern.

- First, coastal state claims that restrict the exercise of high seas freedoms may continue to increase. These may take the form of new restrictions on navigation, overflight, and military activities within 200 miles or of new claims to control areas beyond 200 miles.

- Second, neither the United States nor the Soviet Union may resist this continued erosion of high seas freedoms any more consistently and effectively than in the past. (Japan is even more unlikely to do so, and the European Common Market shows signs of regarding its primary maritime interests as coastal rather than global.)

- Third, the United States itself may continue to make broad coastal state claims that in principle—although perhaps not in precise legal detail—contradict its interest in stability and principled respect for the freedoms of the seas.

The question is not whether a law of the sea convention is a substitute for an effective long-range policy for dealing with these problems. It is not. The question is whether express widespread adherence to identical statements of the underlying principles and rules, and unified procedures for interpreting them in a treaty, would substantially affect the vigor and effectiveness of such a long-range policy. In the short run, the enthusiasm for demonstrating that we do not need the new treaty may well invigorate that policy. But what of the longer haul?

The Third UN Conference on the Law of the Sea will recede into history. Attitudes toward the convention it produced may cease to be the immediate issue. But the problems of the law of the sea will remain and evolve. Any country that considers itself a global maritime power must recognize that the basic problems are essentially global, not national or regional. Sooner or later, they will have to be resolved on a global basis.

The challenge to American will, interests, and leadership is found not only, or even principally, in frustrating rhetorical confrontations in the UN and other multilateral bodies. If the law of the sea teaches any lesson, it is that in daily encounters with coastal nations around the globe the United States must be prepared to deal effectively and unromantically with the few who wish us ill and the many who have priorities that differ from and may conflict with our own.

When the work and hoopla of defining a national oceans policy are over and emotions have settled, it will be the task of the serious-minded to formulate and execute an international oceans strategy for the United States in a political and legal environment that is far from benign. That strategy will, as it must, include an effort to build common global understandings regarding the rules of the game. If not in form, then in fact, the point of departure will be the 1982 convention.

V

Appendix

APPENDIX

BERNARD H. OXMAN

Summary of the Law of the Sea Convention

After fifteen years of treaty negotiations, a new United Nations Convention on the Law of the Sea[1] was opened for signature in Jamaica on 10 December 1982. Although President Reagan found that most provisions "are consistent with U.S. interests" and "serve well the interests of all nations," he, along with the governments of Great Britain, Italy, Luxembourg, and West Germany, declined to authorize signature of the convention because of its deep seabed mining provisions. The five other members of the European Common Market, most other Western countries, the Soviet bloc, China, and most African, Asian, and Latin American countries were among the 117 signatories on 10 December. Japan joined them a few weeks later, and more signatures are likely.

This essay appeared in slightly different form as "The New Law of the Sea" in the *Journal of the American Bar Association* 69 (February 1983), p. 156. Copyright © 1983, American Bar Association. Used by permission.

There is a substantial possibility that more than the necessary 60 signatories will ratify the convention and bring it into force in this decade.

Except perhaps for the provisions on deep seabed mining and the settlement of disputes, the stipulations of the convention are already regarded by some government and private experts as generally authoritative statements of existing customary international law applicable to all states. The president of the conference, however, joined many other delegates in warning that other countries will not necessarily accord Americans their *quids* if the U.S. government stays out and denies others their *quos*.

There are many facets to the current debate regarding the convention, a treaty of some 200 single-spaced pages whose 446 articles describe the basic rights and duties of states in connection with all activities at sea. Broad issues of process, principle, and precedent are invoked with respect to matters as varied as defense, ecology, economics, ethics, oceanography, politics, and (sometimes) law. Many of these issues are enunciated in other contributions to this collection.

It is not my purpose here to rehearse the debate but merely to give a brief summary of its object: the convention. Still, every sentence and omission reflects some professional judgment with which others might reasonably differ.

History of Negotiations

As its title indicates, the nine-year-long Third UN Conference on the Law of the Sea was not the first effort to lay down the rules of the law of the sea by universal agreement. Efforts to codify the law of the sea began under the League of Nations, culminating in the adoption by the first UN conference of four conventions on the law of the sea in 1958. Although ratified by the United States and many other maritime countries, the 1958 conventions did not fully achieve the objectives of a modern, universally respected body of law. Negotiated before almost half the current community of nations won independence, they were not ratified by a substantial majority of states, failed to resolve certain important issues, and did not deal adequately with certain new problems. The second conference was called in 1960 to try again to fix a maximum limit for the territorial sea. Its failure, coupled with the breakdown of customary restraint in maritime claims, meant that there remained no sufficiently reliable basis for predicting or restraining the increasingly conflicting claims of states to use and control the sea.

The third conference was charged by the UN General Assembly in 1973 with preparing a new comprehensive convention on the law of the sea, by consensus if at all possible. Beginning in 1975, the officers of the conference combined texts and ideas that emerged from informal negotiations and submitted them as an informal negotiating text at the end of a session. Delegations returned to the next session with a clearer idea of what they were prepared to accept. The final text emerged from the eighth iteration in this process. The few substantive amendments pressed to a vote were defeated.

Following the U.S. request for a record vote, on 30 April 1982 the conference adopted the text by a vote of 130 delegations in favor[2] and 4 against,[3] including the United States, with 18 abstentions[4] and 18 unrecorded.[5] Many Western European countries abstained on the vote because they preferred further improvements in the deep seabed mining provisions and were urged by the U.S. to vote no. Eastern European countries abstained because they were miffed by a technical provision in the conference resolution on protection of preconvention mining investments that they felt discriminated in favor of U.S. companies.

The Legal Map of the Sea

The convention applies to the "sea." Oceans, gulfs, bays, and seas are part of the "sea"; lakes and rivers are not. It has long been accepted that the sea may not be claimed in the same manner as land areas. Some parts are allocated to adjacent coastal states, and the rest is open to all.

The convention seeks to accommodate the interests of a state in two ways. First, it gives each state and its nationals freedom to act in pursuit of those interests (e.g., navigation rights and high seas freedoms). Second, the treaty limits the freedom of others to act in a manner adverse to those interests. Thus it imposes a duty on foreign states and their nationals to act in a prescribed manner (e.g., with respect to safety and environmental restrictions), and it gives a state the right to prevent or control activities of foreign states and their nationals (e.g., to maintain territorial sovereignty or coastal state jurisdiction over mining or fishing). Because rules generally apply to all, states must balance their desire to maximize their own freedom of action with their desire to limit the freedom of action of others. Law is one way to achieve this balance.

Internal waters. Not only lakes and rivers but also harbors and other parts of the sea are so much enclosed by the land that they are, in effect, internal. An example is a small bay. Emergencies aside, use of internal waters (including their seabed and airspace) generally requires coastal state consent. However, because they are more open and useful to navigation, in those internal waters established by a "system of straight baselines" connecting coastal or insular promontories, foreign states enjoy the same passage rights as in the territorial sea. The convention contains a number of technical rules on how to establish baselines delimiting internal waters. These are largely drawn from the 1958 Territorial Sea Convention.

One innovative provision permits a state to investigate and try foreign ships visiting its ports for discharging pollutants in violation of international rules and standards virtually anywhere at sea.

The territorial sea. Every coastal state is entitled to exercise sovereignty over a belt of sea adjacent to the coast, including its seabed and airspace. This "territorial sea" is measured seaward from the coast or baselines delimiting internal waters.

One of the reasons for calling the third conference was that the earlier two conferences failed to reach agreement on the maximum permissible breadth of the territorial sea and, accordingly, on the extent of the free high seas. Respect for the old 3-mile limit had eroded. Some territorial sea claims extended as far as 200 miles. The new convention establishes 12 nautical miles as the maximum permissible breadth of the territorial sea.

The sovereignty of the coastal state in the territorial sea is subject to a right of "innocent passage" for foreign ships, but not for aircraft or submerged submarines. The question of what constitutes "innocence," as well as the extent of coastal state regulatory power over ships in passage, remained in dispute following the 1958 conference. While repeating the provisions of the 1958 convention on innocent passage, the new convention adds a list of activities that are not innocent passage, prohibits discrimination based on the flag or destination of a ship, and clarifies the right of the coastal state to establish sealanes and traffic separation schemes and to control pollution.

Straits. Any extension of the geographic area in which a coastal state exercises sovereignty at sea reduces the area in which the freedoms of the sea, including freedom of navigation and overflight, may be exercised. In narrow straits, extension of the territorial sea or the establishment of straight baselines may eliminate any (or any usable) high seas passage through the area. At the same time, states bordering straits may be subject to political pressures to assert control over transit for military, economic, or environmental purposes.

Under the 1958 convention, a coastal state could not suspend innocent passage in straits used for international navigation. The new convention establishes a more liberal right of "transit passage" for aircraft and submerged submarines as well as surface ships in most straits, including Bab-el-Mandeb, Dover, Gibraltar, Hormuz, and Malacca. The debate about whether warship passage is "innocent" is rendered irrelevant. There is no right to stop a ship in transit passage, unless a merchant ship's violation of internationally approved regulations threatens major damage to the marine environment of the strait.

Special long-standing treaty regimes for particular straits (such as the Turkish straits), rights under the peace treaty between Egypt and Israel, and the regulation of artificial canals are unaffected by the convention.

Archipelagic waters. The new convention generally validates the sovereignty claims of some independent island nations (e.g., the Bahamas, Indonesia, and the Philippines) over all waters within their archipelagos, subject to a right of "archipelagic sealanes passage," similar to transit passage, through the archipelago for all ships and aircraft, including submerged submarines. Specific

criteria are established for limiting the situations in which
archipelagic baselines may be drawn around an island group and
how far they may extend.

The contiguous zone. The coastal state may take enforcement
measures in a contiguous zone adjacent to its territorial sea to prevent or punish infringement of its customs, fiscal, immigration, or
sanitary laws in its territory or territorial sea. The new convention
extends the 1958 limit of this contiguous zone from 12 to 24 nautical miles from the coast or baseline. It also permits the coastal
state to take special measures to protect archeological treasures.

The continental shelf. It is now generally accepted that the
coastal state has exclusive "sovereign rights" to explore and exploit the natural resources of the seabed and subsoil of the continental shelf adjacent to its coast and seaward of its territorial sea.
The questions are where and for what other activities coastal
state authorization is needed.

The new convention permits the coastal state to establish the
permanent outer limit of its continental shelf at either 200 nautical miles from the coast or baseline, or at the outer edge of the continental margin (the submerged prolongation of the land mass),
whichever is further seaward. Its elaborate criteria for locating
the edge of the continental margin are designed to allocate virtually all seabed oil and gas to coastal states. Once approved by an
international commission of experts, the coastal state's charts
showing the location of the outer edge of its continental margin
are final and binding on the rest of the world (or at least on the
other parties to the convention). This *ex parte* procedure is intended to lower the risk of investment in a manner similar to the
common law action to quiet title.

Under the new convention, the coastal state has sovereign
rights over the natural resources of the seabed and subsoil of the
continental shelf, as well as the exclusive right to authorize and
regulate drilling for all purposes and the right to consent to the
course for pipelines. The coastal state's newly elaborated rights
regarding installations and marine scientific research on the continental shelf are generally the same as its rights concerning the
exclusive economic zone discussed in the next section.

The new convention specifies three new duties of the coastal state. The first, applicable to the entire continental shelf, requires every coastal state to establish environmental standards for all activities and installations under its jurisdiction that are no less effective than those contained in international standards. At the same time, the rigid petroleum installation removal regulations of the 1958 convention have been relaxed in response to oil company concerns.

The other new duties are applicable only to that part of the continental shelf that is seaward of 200 nautical miles from the coast. One requires the coastal state to pay a small percentage of the value of mineral production from the area into an international fund to be distributed to parties to the convention, particularly developing countries. Another prohibits the coastal state from withholding consent for marine scientific research outside specific areas under development.

The exclusive economic zone. The provisions on the exclusive economic zone (EEZ) are all new law. Measured by any yardstick — political, military, economic, scientific, environmental, or recreational — the overwhelming proportion of activities and interests in the sea are affected by this new regime.

Under the convention every coastal state has the right to establish an exclusive economic zone seaward of its territorial sea and extending up to 200 nautical miles from its coast or baseline. Seabed areas beyond the territorial sea and within 200 miles of the coast are therefore subject to both the continental shelf and economic zone regimes.

Two separate sets of rights exist in the economic zone: those enjoyed exclusively by the coastal state and those that may be exercised by all states. The division is by activity, not by area or ship.

The rights of the coastal state in the economic zone are:

- exclusive sovereign rights for the purpose of exploring, exploiting, conserving, and managing the living and nonliving natural resources of both the waters and the seabed and subsoil;

- exclusive sovereign rights to control other activities for the economic exploitation and exploration of the zone, such as the production of energy from the water, currents, and winds;

- the exclusive right to control the construction and use of all artificial islands and those installations and structures that are used for economic purposes or that may interfere with the coastal state's exercise of its rights in the zone (e.g., an oil rig or offshore tanker depot);

- the right to be informed of and participate in proposed marine scientific research projects, and to withhold consent for a project in a timely manner under specified circumstances;

- the right to control dumping of wastes;

- the right to board, inspect, and, when there is threat of major damage, arrest a merchant ship suspected of discharging pollutants in the zone in violation of internationally approved standards. This right is subject to substantial safeguards to protect shippers, sailors, and consumers. Even if investigation of the ship indicates a violation, it must be released promptly on reasonable bond. If release is not obtained within ten days, an international court may set the bond and order release "without delay." If so authorized, a private party may seek this release order on behalf of the flag state. The convention establishes a time limit for prosecution, requires that the coastal state observe "recognized rights of the accused," prohibits punishments other than monetary fines, and restricts successive trials by different states for the same offense.

The rights of all states in the economic zone are:

- the high seas freedoms of navigation, overflight, and the laying of submarine cables and pipelines;

- other internationally lawful uses of the sea related to these freedoms, such as those associated with the operation of ships, aircraft, and submarine cables and pipelines. This category may cover a gamut of uses such as recreational swimming, weather monitoring, and various naval operations.

This allocation of rights is accompanied by extensive duties.

Because both the coastal state and other states have independent rights to use the economic zone, each is required to ensure that its rights are exercised with "due regard" to the rights and duties of the other.

Flag states must ensure that their ships observe generally accepted international anti-pollution regulations, and each coastal state must take measures to ensure that activities under its jurisdiction or control do not cause pollution damage to other states.

The coastal state is required to ensure the conservation of living resources in the waters of the economic zone. Except with respect to marine mammals, it must also promote their optimum utilization by determining its harvesting capacity and granting access under reasonable conditions to foreign vessels to fish for the surplus, if any, that remains under its conservation limits. Neighboring states with small enclosed coastlines, or none at all, enjoy some priority of access to this surplus. International protection of whales and other marine mammals is required, as is regional regulation of highly migratory species such as tuna.

If the economic zones or continental shelves of neighboring coastal states overlap, they are to be delimited by agreement between those states on the basis of international law in order to achieve an equitable solution. This general provision should be read against the background of an increasing number of bilateral agreements and international judicial and arbitral decisions on offshore boundary delimitation.

The high seas. Like the 1958 Convention on the High Seas, the new convention does not contain an exhaustive list of the freedoms of the high seas. Both expressly name the freedoms of navigation, overflight, fishing, and laying of submarine cables and pipelines. The new convention also lists freedom of scientific research and freedom to construct artificial islands and other installations permitted under international law.

Largely copied from the 1958 convention, the new high seas regime has been augmented by stronger safety and environmental obligations of the flag state and special provisions on the suppression of pirate broadcasting and illicit traffic in drugs. Freedom to fish on the high seas is subject to specific conservation and ecological requirements. Free high seas fishing is eliminated for salmon and can be eliminated or restricted for whales and other marine mammals.

Unlike the 1958 convention, the new convention does not contain a definition of the high seas. Rather it says that its articles on the high seas apply to all parts of the sea beyond the economic zone, and that most of those high seas articles also apply within the economic zone to the extent they are not incompatible with the articles on the economic zone. Thus, for example, the law of nationality of ships and the law of piracy continue unchanged in the economic zone.

The international seabed area. The "international seabed area" comprises the seabed and subsoil "beyond the limits of national jurisdiction"—that is, in effect, beyond the limits of the economic zone and continental shelf subject to coastal state jurisdiction. This area is declared to be the "common heritage of mankind." Its principal resource of current interest consists of polymetallic nodules lying at or near the surface of the deep ocean beds, particularly in the Pacific and to a lesser degree in the Indian Ocean. The nodules contain nickel, manganese, cobalt, copper, and traces of other metals.

Nonresource uses, including scientific research, are free, and prospecting is almost as free. On the other hand, mining requires a contract from an International Seabed Authority. Parties to the convention are prohibited from recognizing mineral rights asserted outside the convention system.

To obtain a contract conferring the exclusive right to explore and mine a particular area with security of tenure for a fixed term of years, a company must be "sponsored" by a state party. It must propose two mining areas, one to be awarded to the company, the other to be "reserved" by the Seabed Authority for exploration and exploitation by its own commercial mining company, the Enterprise, or by a developing country.

Assuming procedural requirements are met, the Seabed Authority may refuse to issue the contract to a qualified applicant in essentially four circumstances:

- if the applicant has a poor record of compliance under a previous contract;

- if the particular area has been closed to mining because of special environmental problems;

- if a single sponsoring state would thereby acquire more active minesites, particularly in the same general area, than are permissible under fairly broad geographic limits;

- if there is already a contract or application for all or part of the same area.

Before beginning commercial production, a miner must obtain a production authorization. This must be issued so long as the aggregate authorized production from the international seabed area would not exceed a twenty-year interim ceiling. In the absence of an applicable commodity agreement, this restriction limits the total nodule production to an amount that would generate by any given year no more than the cumulative increase in world demand for nickel in the five years before the first commercial production, plus 60 percent of the cumulative projected increase in total world demand for nickel thereafter.

In exchange for mining rights in a contract that may not be modified without its agreement, the mining company assumes three basic obligations:

- It must abide by various performance, safety, environmental, and other technical ground rules.

- It must pay to the Seabed Authority a specified proportion of the value of production or, at its election, a smaller proportion of production coupled with a specified proportion of profits. The Seabed Authority must use the funds to cover its administrative expenses and may then distribute the remainder to developing countries and peoples designated by regulation.

- Until ten years after the Enterprise first begins commercial production, the company must be willing to sell to the Enterprise, on fair and reasonable commercial terms and conditions determined by agreement or commercial arbitration, mining (but not processing) technology being used at the site if equivalent technology is not available on the open market. Alternatively, it would have the same obligation to a developing country planning to exploit the "reserved" site submitted by that company.

The International Seabed Authority. The Authority would have the standard structure of an intergovernmental organization—an

Assembly of all states parties, a Council of limited membership, and a Secretariat.

The thirty-six-member Council must include four of the largest consumers and four of the largest (land-based) producers of the types of resources produced from the deep seabed, as well as four of the states whose nationals have made the largest investment in deep seabed mining. The Soviet bloc obtained an express guarantee of three Council seats in exchange for tacitly conceding at least seven, and probably eight or nine, seats to the West, including a guaranteed seat for the largest consumer, which was intended to be the United States should it become a party. Developing countries will hold most of the remaining seats.

The Assembly is referred to as the supreme organ of the Seabed Authority. However, the adoption of legally binding mining rules and regulations, restrictive environmental orders, and proposed amendments to the deep seabed mining provisions of the convention requires a consensus decision of the Council. Other substantive decisions, depending on their importance, require a three-fourths or two-thirds vote in the Council. A Technical Commission is required to recommend Council approval of applications for mining contracts if they satisfy the relevant requirements of the convention and the rules and regulations. That recommendation may be rejected only by consensus, excluding the applicant's sponsoring state.

The Enterprise—an intergovernmental mining company—is the most unusual feature of the Seabed Authority. The initial capitalization target for the Enterprise is the cost of developing one minesite, now estimated at well over $1 billion. Half would be in the form of private loans guaranteed by the states parties and half in the form of interest-free loans from the states parties.

If Jamaica ratifies the convention, it would be the site of the International Seabed Authority.

General Obligations under the Convention

The convention specifies a number of duties that apply to all or most of the sea. The most developed are the strong new duties to protect and preserve the marine environment. There are also duties to promote marine scientific research and dissemination of scientific knowledge, to protect archeological treasures found at sea, to use the seas for peaceful purposes, to refrain from any threat or use of force contrary to the UN Charter, and to settle disputes peacefully. There is a special chapter guaranteeing land-locked states access to the sea. Abuse of rights is prohibited.

Settlement of disputes. The convention is the first global treaty of its kind to require, without a right of reservation, that an unresolved dispute between states parties concerning its interpretation or application shall be submitted at the request of either party to arbitration or adjudication for a decision binding on the other party. There are, however, important exceptions to this rule:

- Disputes concerning the rights of the coastal state in the economic zone or the continental shelf may be submitted by another state only in cases of interference with navigation, overflight, the laying of submarine cables and pipelines, and related rights, or in cases of violation of specified international environmental standards.

- Disputes regarding historic bays and maritime boundary delimitation between states with opposite or adjacent coasts, disputes concerning military activities, and disputes that are before the UN Security Council may be excluded by unilateral declaration.

Arbitration is the applicable procedure unless:

- emergency measures (e.g., vessel release) are necessary before an arbitration panel has been constituted;

- both the "defendant" and the "plaintiff" have accepted the jurisdiction of the International Court of Justice in The Hague or the new Tribunal on the Law of the Sea, to be established in Hamburg if West Germany ratifies the treaty; or

- the dispute concerns exploration or exploitation of the resources of the international seabed area. In this event, the case may be brought to a chamber of the Tribunal on the Law of the Sea or commercial arbitration, depending on the circumstances. These forums are open both to states parties and to the deep seabed mining companies sponsored by them.

Conference Resolutions

A Preparatory Commission of treaty signatories will draft provisional deep seabed mining regulations that will, in effect, interpret, clarify, and apply the convention text with greater precision. Only when they are drafted will one be able to know the exact nature of a miner's rights and obligations under the deep seabed mining system and the mining contracts to be issued. These regulations will automatically enter into force with the convention a year after 60 states have ratified it.

A conference resolution authorizes the Preparatory Commission to register the deep seabed mining companies that made substantial investments before 1983 as pioneer investors, each with the exclusive right to carry out exploration and testing in a registered area of 150,000 square kilometers at the start. Once the convention enters into force, a qualified pioneer investor sponsored by a state party must be granted a mining contract for that half of the original registered area selected by the investor if the Preparatory Commission has certified compliance with the conference resolution.

France, Great Britain, the United States, and West Germany signed an agreement in 1982 to deal with exploration applications for overlapping areas previously filed under their respective deep seabed mining laws. Such an agreement is envisaged by and consistent with the conference resolution on pioneer investment. It also may be regarded as a first step in establishing an international arrangement for deep seabed mining outside or in lieu of the convention.

Reservation, Amendment, and Withdrawal

The convention does not permit reservations, but does permit other declarations and statements. Amendment is possible, but difficult—perhaps a bit less so with respect to deep seabed mining.

The deep seabed mining system as a whole is subject to review fifteen years after commercial production of deep seabed minerals begins. Should the review conference be unable to reach agreement on amendments within five years after it is convened, it may adopt amendments to the mining system by a three-fourths vote. These would enter into force for all parties a year after ratification by three-fourths of the parties, but would not affect mining under contracts already issued.

A party has the right to withdraw from the convention at any time on one year's notice.

Notes

Contributors

Index

NOTES

1. David D. Caron: "Reconciling Domestic Principles and International Cooperation"

1. In 1930, the League of Nations convened a Conference for the Codification of International Law. The conference was unable to reach a consensus on its law of the sea concerns, however. See 1 League of Nations, "Acts of the Conference for the Codification of International Law," pp. 123–37 and 165–69 (UN Doc. C.351.M.145.1930.V). Later, the United Nations convened conferences on the law of the sea in 1958 and in 1960, but although both made contributions, neither solved the problem of unilateral claims by coastal states to extended ocean jurisdiction. As to the 1958 convention, see Phillip Jessup, "The United Nations Conference on the Law of the Sea," *Columbia Law Review* 50 (1959): 234. As to the 1960 convention, see Arthur Dean, "Second Geneva Conference on the Law of the Sea," *American Journal of International Law* 54 (1960): 751.

2. John Stevenson and Bernard Oxman, "The Third United Nations Conference on the Law of the Sea: The 1974 Caracas Session," *American Journal of International Law* 69 (1975): 1, 30.

3. See U.S. Department of State Bulletin 74, 1976, p. 539.

4. See J. N. Barkenbus, *Deep Seabed Resources: Politics and Technology* (New York: Free Press, 1979).

5. Bernard Oxman, "The Third United Nations Conference on the Law of the Sea: The Tenth Session," *American Journal of International Law* 76 (1982): 1.

6. David Caron, "Municipal Legislation for Exploitation of the Deep Seabed," *Ocean Development and International Law Journal* 8 (1980): 261.

7. See Gunther Weissberg, "International Law Meets the Short Term National Interest: The Maltese Proposal on the Sea-Bed and the Ocean Floor—Its Fate in Two Cities," *International and Comparative Law Quarterly* 18 (1969): 41.

8. Northcutt Ely, "Deep Seabed Mining: Congress Steams to the Rescue," *International Lawyer* 10 (1976): 537, quoting from Daniel Moynihan, "The United States in Opposition," *Commentary* 59 (March 1975): 41.

9. See John Breaux, "The Diminishing Prospects for an Acceptable Law of the Sea Treaty," *Virginia Journal of International Law* 19 (1979): 257; and Richard Darman, "The Law of the Sea: Rethinking U.S. Interests," *Foreign Affairs* 56 (1978): 373.

10. See United Nations, General Assembly, *Declaration on the Establishment of a New International Economic Order,* G.A. Res. 3201, 6th Spec. Sess., Suppl. (A/9559), May 1974.

11. See Oxman, p. 2.

12. Statement by Mr. Inam Ul-Haque (Pakistan) on behalf of the Group of 77, Informal Plenary, 10 August 1981.

13. This idea is often couched in the maxim *"Ubi societas, ibi ius"* (where there is a community there is a legal order). As to Cicero's ideas, see his *De Re Publica, De Legibus,* and *De Officiis.*

2. Arvid Pardo: "An Opportunity Lost"

1. UN Doc. A/CONF 62/122, 7 October 1982.

2. "The outer limits of the continental shelf on the seabed . . . either shall not exceed 350 nautical miles from the baselines from which the breadth of the territorial sea is measured or shall not exceed 100 nautical miles from the 2,500-metre isobath." Ibid., Article 76 (5).

3. For instance, "the Governments of the Republic of Indonesia and of Malaysia agreed that the straits of Malacca and Singapore are not international straits, while fully recognizing their use for international shipping. . . ." (joint statement of the Governments of Indonesia, Malaysia, and Singapore, 16 November 1971).

4. Many questions concerning military uses of the marine environment are unresolved and could give rise to serious incidents. The legality of the following, among other activities, is controversial:

  (a) establishment of security zones beyond the territorial sea;
  (b) exclusion of foreign shipping from large areas of the high seas that have been unilaterally reserved for security purposes;
  (c) emplacement of anti-submarine warfare devices on the legal continental shelf of another state without the latter's knowledge or consent, etc.

5. See 1958 Geneva Convention on the High Seas, Article 25.

6. See, for instance, James Bridgman, Paper no. 3, Villanova Colloquium on Peace, Justice and the Law of the Sea, 1977.

7. The absurdities quoted, and several others that could be quoted, derive largely from the disingenuous definition of islands contained in Article 121.of the convention read in conjunction with Part IV (Archipelagic States).

8. The 200-nautical-mile exclusive economic zone, however, should be measured from the coast or from straight baselines, the length of which is strictly limited. This is not the case in the present convention, which permits baseline manipulation (and hence further extension of coastal state jurisdiction) since, *inter alia,* no limit is set on the length of straight baselines (see Article 7, particularly paragraphs (1), (2), and (5)).

9. Thus, for instance, Article 239 obligates states to "promote and facilitate the development and conduct of marine scientific research," which is the indispensable prerequisite to rational resource management. Within the exclusive economic zone "the coastal state, taking into account the best scientific evidence available to it, shall ensure through proper conservation and management measures that the maintenance of the living resources . . . is not endangered by over-exploitation" (Article 61 (2)), and states are enjoined to cooperate with each other and with "competent" international organizations to this end. Beyond national jurisdiction "all states have the duty to take . . . such measures for their respective nationals as may be necessary for the conservation of the living resources of the high seas" (Article 117; see also Article 119), an obligation identical to the one already affirmed in the 1958 Geneva Convention on Fisheries (Article 1 (2)), and elaborate provision is made for international management of the mineral resources of the seabed beyond national jurisdiction.

10. Thus the general obligation to promote marine scientific research is followed by a specific provision subjecting marine scientific research "of direct significance for the exploration and exploitation of natural resources" to a discretionary consent regime that may inhibit research (Article 246 (5) (a)); the general duty of the coastal state to ensure that the maintenance of the living resources of the exclusive economic zone is not endangered by over-exploitation is heavily qualified by the fact that the coastal state establishes the allowable

catch virtually at its discretion. The approach to problems of marine living resource management is well illustrated by Article 63 (2), which reads, "where the same stock or stocks of associated species occur both within the exclusive economic zone and in an area beyond and adjacent to the zone, the coastal state and the states fishing for such stocks in the adjacent area shall seek either directly or through appropriate subregional or regional organizations to agree upon the measures necessary for the conservation of these stocks *in the adjacent area.*" In short, the coastal state may exercise unfettered discretion with regard to conservation measures in marine areas under national jurisdiction.

11. See Convention, Annex II, Article 4, read in conjunction with Article 8.

12. Under a previous version of the convention (UN Doc A/CONF 62/WP 10/Rev 3, Article 134), the Authority was to have been notified by the coastal states concerned of the limits of the Area and was required to register and publish the notifications received; now even these vestigial functions have been taken away.

13. Article 136 reads as follows: "The *Area* and its resources are a common heritage of mankind."

14. Production controls were supposed to protect developing countries that produce minerals contained in the nodules "from adverse effects on their economies or on their export earnings resulting from a reduction in the price of an affected mineral or in the volume of that mineral exported. . . ." Instead, the production controls envisaged in the convention, which are based on the quantity of nickel expected to be produced from manganese nodules, protect mainly developed countries, such as Canada, from possible future competition (see Article 151). Few developing countries are major nickel producers. Second, commercially exploitable manganese nodule deposits are found on the legal continental shelf, as defined by Article 76, of some states. Production controls governing only the international area and not also marine areas under national jurisdiction can only weaken the slim competitive chances of the Authority.

15. See UN Doc A/CONF 62/L 65.

16. The Council is the central organ of the future Authority with regard to the exploration and exploitation of manganese nodules. It is "the executive organ of the Authority having the power to establish . . . the specific policies to be pursued by the Authority on any questions within the competence of the Authority" (Article 162). In this vital organ, where states with violently opposed interests and ideologies are represented, decisions will be taken by majorities, ranging from a simple majority in procedural questions to a consensus for the most important questions. It seems rather optimistic under the circumstances to expect timely and appropriate decisions on important questions.

17. Resolution I establishes a Preparatory Commission (a) to prepare draft rules, regulations, and procedures to enable the future International Seabed Authority to commence its functions; (b) to exercise the powers assigned to it under Resolution II; (c) "to undertake studies on the problems which would be encountered by developing land-based producers likely to be most seriously affected by production in the Area. . . ."; (d) to perform traditional preparatory functions, such as drafting a budget. Resolution II guarantees that a limited number of "pioneer investors" will obtain manganese nodule exploitation contracts and production authorizations from the future Authority under certain conditions.

18. See, for instance, Article 7(2), 47(2), 47(8).

19. *United States Policy for the Seabed,* U.S. Department of State Bulletin 737 (1970).

3. Leigh S. Ratiner: "The Costs of American Rigidity"

1. In addition to government agencies, all of the representatives of the American ocean mining groups were invited to participate fully in the work of the delegation; special efforts were organized to obtain the views of companies not able to be in New York, in advance of the delegation's accepting any compromises.

2. Article 137, paragraph 3, of the treaty prohibits states from recognizing seabed mining claims that are not derived from the treaty and its rules and regulations. Under customary international law principles of treaty interpretation, a state that signs a treaty is bound not to act incompatibly with it pending its ratification and entry into force.

3. In addition, coastal state rights to control offshore pollution as well as shipping state rights within coastal waters are covered by the treaty. The rights of marine scientific researchers and coastal states are also set forth. Space does not permit an exhaustive listing of the hundreds of legal rights and obligations that create the overall balance of sea law in the treaty. Suffice it to say that virtually all uses of the oceans are affected by the legal rights and obligations set out therein.

4.   W. Scott Burke and Frank S. Brokaw: "Ideology and the Law of the Sea"

1. Among the basic tenets of the NIEO are fifteen fundamentals of international economic relations that, according to the United Nations Charter of Economic Rights and Duties of States, "shall" govern international economic and political relations. They include the right of each state to nationalize foreign private investments according to such laws and regulations the state considers pertinent; the right of every state to benefit from scientific and technological developments for its social and economic advancement; the right to establish "organizations of primary commodity producers;" and the corresponding duty of all states to "respect that right by refraining from applying economic and political measures that would limit it."

2. Quoted in Peter Bauer and John O'Sullivan, "Ordering the World About: The New International Economic Order," *Policy Review* 1 (Summer 1977): 56. President Nyerere's statement is grounded on the premise that the economic process is a zero-sum game. A zero-sum model focuses on the distribution of an existing stock of wealth rather than on the conditions needed to create an increased flow of economic value. It assumes that any person's gain equals another person's loss. Many Third World leaders who accept this view may have mistakenly inferred this paradigm from the process of the seizure of political power, where it is certainly valid.

3. *Business Week,* 7 February 1983, p. 52.

4. *The Wall Street Journal,* 7 February 1983, p. 9:

"The administration, concerned about international financial strains, is beginning to explore new, more striking measures to help developing countries avert defaulting on their debts.

"Although the discussions still are preliminary, a high-level task force is considering proposals under which Western governments would take over a portion of poor countries' debt burdens and refinance them on easier terms.

"At the same time, under these ideas, private international banks would be forced to assume greater financial losses in cases where borrowing countries couldn't meet their loan repayment schedules and had to stretch out their loans or stop paying the principal. Under current U.S. rules, banks may escape writing such loans off as a loss. . . ."

5. Quoted in Lilliana Torreh-Bayouth, "UNCLOS III: The Remaining Obstacles to Consensus on the Deepsea Mining Regime," *Texas International Law Journal* 16 (1981): 94.

6. Ibid., pp. 84–87.

7. Ibid., p. 99:

"This new idea could be termed Res Unitas Communis: a communis centralized under a regulatory mechanism capable of deciding who has right of access and under what terms and conditions, and capable of barring such access altogether. This trend has taken shape under the new drive of the developing countries for the NIEO. This new order necessitates planned effort and focused development to become viable. A similar term has been invoked in the negotiations for a Moon Treaty to establish a regime for the exploitation of resources in outer space, which area has also been categorized as the Common Heritage of Mankind."

8. While we must always select the ablest and most expert representatives, the choice of such dedicated and energetic negotiators as those who represented the United States at UNCLOS may sometimes work against the national interest. Such men and women spend years striving to achieve the best agreement possible. They tend to become wedded to the outcome and are disposed to argue in its favor; if the terms agreed upon are judged contrary to the national interest, their performance could be viewed as inadequate and the years devoted to the negotiations wasted. This may explain the seductiveness of the negotiating process and the vigor with which its participants defend its outcome.

9. Some treaty advocates claim that the treaty provides for unimpeded passage through straits. If this were unambiguously true, it would be a significant advantage. However, in fact, the treaty is unclear on this point. On its face, the relevant wording of the convention gives the power to determine whether the conditions permitting free passage obtain to straits states, not to the country wishing to pass. Thus transit rights are not conclusively established but remain dependent upon the willingness of the great sea powers to use or threaten force to compel others to accept their interpretations of the treaty. See W. Michael Reisman, "The Regime of Straits and National Security: An Appraisal of International Lawmaking," *American Journal of International Law* 74 (1980): 48.

10. See, e.g., Elliot Richardson, "Power, Mobility and the Law of the Sea," *Foreign Affairs* (Spring 1980): 902, 916; and Leigh S. Ratiner, "The Law of the Sea: A Crossroads for American Foreign Policy," *Foreign Affairs* (Summer 1982): 1006, revised and reprinted in this volume as "The Costs of American Rigidity."

11. See, e.g., U.S. Congress, Senate, *Law of the Sea Negotiations: Hearings Before the Subcommittee on Arms Control, Oceans, International Operations and Environment of the Senate Foreign Relations Committee,* 97th Cong., 1st Sess., 4 June and 30 September 1981, p. 57 (statement of Ms. Lee Kimball, United Methodist Law of the Sea Project), cited hereinafter as *Hearings.*

12. See, e.g., Editorial, "The Reagan Crew at Sea," *The New York Times,* 4 May 1982, p. A30.

13. *Hearings,* p. 44.

14. The United Kingdom, the Federal Republic of Germany, and Italy have apparently decided not to sign the treaty.

15. *Hearings,* p. 64.

16. *Hearings,* p. 67.

17. *Hearings,* p. 72.

18. *Hearings,* p. 77.

19. *The Washington Times,* 20 October 1982, p. 4A.

20. Ibid.

21. Ibid.

22. Paul B. Engo, "A Defense of the Draft Convention," *Journal of Contemporary Studies,* vol. 5, no. 2 (Spring 1982): 92.

23. *Business Week,* 8 November 1982, pp. 43–44.

24. Ibid., p. 44.

5. Robert A. Goldwin: "Common Sense vs. 'The Common Heritage'"

1. " . . . the creation of the International Seabed Authority by the consensus of practically the entire world community (in which the consent of the U.S. must be counted, because it was given at the Conference *and will, I am sure, be given again*). . . ." (Emphasis added.) Elisabeth Mann Borgese, "The Law of the Sea," *Scientific American* (March 1983): 42–49.

2. "Does President Reagan know what he is doing in preparing a final decision not to sign the law of the sea treaty?" *The Washington Post* editorial, 9 July 1982.

3. "The guardians of pure conservative ideology may have won a battle when the United States stood alone at the Law of the Sea Conference, but the United States may lose a very im-

portant war." Leigh Ratiner, "The Law of the Sea: A Crossroads for American Foreign Policy," *Foreign Affairs* 60 (Summer 1982): 1020. Ratiner's essay, revised, appears in this volume as "The Costs of American Rigidity."

4. "If President Reagan understood the realistic prospects . . . he would have had second thoughts about the pursuit of principle over pragmatism." Ratiner, p. 1018. Discourse on this subject has rarely been dispassionate and often descends to vituperative name-calling. A comparatively mild example appeared as a column in *The New York Times* by one Clifton E. Curtis, identified as an attorney with the Center for Law and Social Policy; in it Curtis characterized the Reagan administration as "jingoistic ideologues" suffering from "ideological paranoia," who "should be deep-sixed." The title of his column is the imperious command "Sign the Sea Law Treaty," *The New York Times*, 21 February 1983, p. A17. Mr. Curtis is professionally concerned with control of ocean pollution but he seems less concerned about the consequences of polluting rational discourse.

5. Statement by the President, 9 July 1982, The White House, Office of the Press Secretary (Santa Barbara, Calif.).

6. For a full discussion of "the common heritage of mankind" as an ideological doctrine and the theoretical errors it has led to in the Law of the Sea Treaty negotiations, see my article "Locke and the Law of the Sea," *Commentary* (June 1981): 46–50.

7. I, unfortunately, was not one of them, relying as I did on what others were saying about the factual matters. See my references to "resources worth billions of dollars" and how the world "suffers from a shortage of these metals," ibid.

8. "Manganese Nodule Mining: Background Information," submitted to Special Standing Committee of the House of Commons on the Deep Sea Mining (Temporary Provisions) Bill by Consolidated Gold Fields Limited, Rio Tinto-Zinc Corporation Limited, and BP Petroleum Development Limited, May 1981. Other members of the Kennecott Consortium are Kennecott Corporation (USA), Mitsubishi Corporation (Japan), and Noranda Mines Limited (Canada).

9. Reported in *Financial Times* (London), 6 October 1982, p. 26.

10. "Minesweeping," *The Economist* (London), 11 December 1982, p. 60.

11. Hobart Rowen, "The Ceramic Example," *The Washington Post,* 17 February 1983, p. A19.

12. "Manganese Nodule Mining: Background Information."

13. "Declining commodity prices made the resource-exporting developing countries wary of a new source of competition for their native ones. Against the opposition of the North (with the exception of Canada) these countries became more interested in limiting production from the seabed than in managing it." Borgese, p. 47.

14. C. R. Tinsley, "The Financing of Deep-Sea Mining," unpublished paper for a conference on U.S. Interests in the Law of the Sea, American Enterprise Institute, October 1981.

15. "There exists no politician in India daring enough to attempt to explain to the masses that cows can be eaten." Indira Gandhi, talking to Oriana Fallaci, quoted in *The Quotable Woman, 1800–1981,* ed. Elaine Partnow; from a book review by Edmund Fuller, *The Wall Street Journal,* 28 March 1983, p. 22.

16. Borgese, p. 47.

6.   Lance N. Antrim and James K. Sebenius: "Incentives for Ocean Mining under the Convention"

1. United Nations General Assembly Resolution 2749, 25 U.N. GAOR, Suppl. No. 280, 24 U.N. Doc. A/8028 (1970).

2. An elaboration of the point that nonseabed issues drove U.S. policy is contained in Richard G. Darman, "The Law of the Sea: Rethinking U.S. Interests," *Foreign Affairs* 56 (1978): 373–95.

3. J. D. Nyhart, L. Antrim, A. Capstaff, A. Kohler, and D. Leshaw, *A Cost Model of Ocean*

Mining and Associated Regulatory Issues, MIT Sea Grant Report MITSG 78–4 (Cambridge, Mass.: MIT, 1978), hereafter cited as "the MIT model."

4. For example, see Arthur D. Little, Inc., "Technological and Economic Assessment of Manganese Nodule Mining and Processing," prepared for the Department of the Interior (Stock no. 024–000–00842–B) (Washington, D.C.: U.S. Govt. Printing Office, 1977), recently summarized and updated in H. Enzer, "Economic Assessment of Ocean Mining," presented at the joint meeting of the Institute for Mining and Metallurgy, the Society of Mining Engineers of AIME, and the Metallurgical Society of the AIME, London, England, May 1980. See also Charles River Associates, Inc., "Analysis of Major Policy Issues Raised by the Commercial Development of Ocean Manganese Nodules," CRA Report no. 383 (Cambridge, Mass.: National Science Foundation, 1981).

5. For a discussion and numerous references to this phenomenon, see David Lax and James K. Sebenius, "Insecure Contracts and Resource Development," *Public Policy* 29 (1981): 417–36.

6. For a description of the overall functioning of the financial provisions from the standpoints of the Authority and the miners, see James K. Sebenius and Mati L. Pal, "Evolving Terms of Mineral Agreements: Risk, Rewards, and Participation in Deep Seabed Mining," *Columbia Journal of World Business* (Winter 1980): 75–83.

7. See, for example, M. Bucovestskey, M. Gillis, and Louis Wells, "Comparative Mining Taxes," in *Taxation and Mining,* ed. M. Gillis (Cambridge, Mass.: Ballinger, 1978), pp. 121–79.

8. J. D. Corrick, *Nickel—1977,* Department of the Interior Bureau of Mines (Washington, D.C.: U.S. Govt. Printing Office, 1977).

9. Science Applications, Inc., *Alternatives for Technology Transfer to the Enterprise,* SAI Report no. SAI–460–80–40ILJ (La Jolla, Calif.: Science Applications, 1978), p. 61.

10. David Smith and Louis Wells, *Negotiating Third World Mineral Agreements: Promises as Prologue* (Cambridge, Mass.: Ballinger, 1975).

11. "Koh: Mining Issues May Go to World Court," *The Interdependent* 8, no. 4 (June/July 1982): 1.

8. Joseph S. Nye, Jr.: "Political Lessons of the New Law of the Sea Regime"

1. These concessions are listed and the prospects assessed in Eliot Marshall, "U.S. Readies for Confrontation on Sea Law," *Science* 215 (19 March 1982).

2. See Leigh S. Ratiner, "The Law of the Sea: A Crossroads for American Foreign Policy," *Foreign Affairs* 60 (Summer 1982): 1006–21, revised and reprinted here as "The Costs of American Rigidity."

3. Elliot Richardson, "Power, Mobility and the Law of the Sea," *Foreign Affairs* 8 (Spring 1980): 918–19.

4. See Robert Keohane and Joseph Nye, *Power and Independence* (Boston: Little, Brown, 1977).

5. See David Deese and Joseph Nye, *Energy and Security* (Cambridge, Mass.: Ballinger, 1981).

APPENDIX.   Bernard H. Oxman: "Summary of the Law of the Sea Convention"

1. UN Doc. A/Conf. 62/122 (1982).

2. Australia, the Bahamas, Brazil, Canada, China, Colombia, Denmark, Egypt, Finland, France, Greece, Iceland, India, Indonesia, Ireland, Japan, Kuwait, Mexico, New Zealand, Nigeria, Norway, Panama, Peru, Saudi Arabia, Sweden, Switzerland, and all other countries except for those listed in footnotes 3, 4, and 5.

3. Israel, Turkey, the United States, and Venezuela. Israel objected to observer status for the PLO. Turkey and Venezuela apparently prefer to resolve offshore boundary disputes with their neighbors before accepting the convention. The United States objected to provisions regarding deep seabed mining.

4. Belgium, Bulgaria, Byelorussian SSR, Czechoslovakia, German Democratic Republic, Federal Republic of Germany, Hungary, Italy, Liberia (initially unrecorded), Luxembourg, Mongolia, Netherlands, Poland, Spain, Thailand, Ukranian SSR, USSR, United Kingdom.

5. Albania, Antigua/Barbuda, Belize, Comoros, Dominica, Ecuador, Equitorial Guinea, Gambia, Holy See, Kiribati, Maldives, Nauru, Solomon Islands, South Africa, Tonga, United Arab Emirates, Vanuatu, Tuvalu.

CONTRIBUTORS

LANCE N. ANTRIM is a project director in the Office of Technology Assessment (OTA) of the U.S. Congress. In 1982 he served as deputy representative on the U.S. delegation to the Law of the Sea Conference. Formerly a policy analyst in the Office of the Secretary of Commerce with responsibility for ocean and mineral issues, he is coauthor of *A Cost Model of Deep Ocean Mining and Associated Regulatory Issues* (1978) and several papers on ocean resource management.

FRANK S. BROKAW is vice-president for corporate banking at Security Pacific National Bank in San Francisco.

CHARLES L. O. BUDERI, a specialist in international business transactions, admiralty issues, and U.S. trade regulations, is currently practicing law in San Francisco.

W. SCOTT BURKE is deputy assistant secretary for human rights and humanitarian affairs at the United States Department of State.

DAVID D. CARON is a lawyer with wide experience in ocean affairs. A graduate of the Coast Guard Academy, he has also served as a navigator and salvage diver in the Arctic and as chief of the Coast Guard Marine Environmental Protection Program for California. Formerly editor-in-chief of *Ecology Law Quarterly* (Boalt Hall School of Law), his most recent publications include "Liability for Transnational Pollution Arising from Offshore Oil Exploitation: A Methodological Approach" *(Ecology Law Quarterly,* 1983) and "Ocean Disposal of Radioactive Wastes: International Law and California" (California Coastal Commission, 1983). Mr. Caron is shortly to assume the post of legal assistant to the Iran–United States Claims Tribunal in The Hague.

LEWIS I. COHEN, a Foreign Service Officer since 1968, is deputy director of the Office of International Commodities and chief of the Marine and Polar Minerals division in the United States Department of State, a post he has held since 1980. He has also served as an international economist for the Bureau of Economic and Business Affairs in the Department of State, as a financial economist at the U.S. Embassy in London, and as an economic officer at the U.S. Embassy in Abijdan, Ivory Coast.

ROBERT A. GOLDWIN is a resident scholar and director of constitutional studies at the American Enterprise Institute, adjunct lecturer at the John F. Kennedy School of Government, Harvard University, and intermittent consultant to the undersecretary of defense for policy. He has taught political science at the University of Chicago and Kenyon College, and was dean of St. John's College in Annapolis. Dr. Goldwin has also served as special advisor to the ambassador, U.S. Mission to the North Atlantic Treaty Organization; in the White House as a special consultant to the president; and in the Pentagon as advisor to the secretary of defense. Some of his recent articles include "Of Men and Angels: A Search for Morality in the Constitution," in *The Moral Foundations of the American Republic* (2nd edition, 1979); "Rights *versus* Duties: No Contest," in *Ethics in Hard Times* (1981); and "Locke and the Law of the Sea" *(Commentary,* June 1981).

JOSEPH S. NYE, JR., professor of government at Harvard University, was from 1977 to 1979 deputy to the undersecretary of state for security assistance, science, and technology. Among his publications is the volume *Power and Independence* (with Robert Keohane, 1977).

BERNARD H. OXMAN, professor of law at the University of Miami School of Law, is a former assistant legal adviser of the Department of State and international lawyer for the U.S. Navy's Judge Advocate General's Corps. He served the Ford, Carter, and Reagan administrations as vice-chairman of the U.S. delegation to the Third UN Conference on the Law of the Sea, and was chairman of the English Language Group of the conference drafting committee. Dr. Oxman is also a member of the Bar of New York and of the District of Columbia.

ARVID PARDO is professor of international relations and senior research fellow at the Institute for Marine and Coastal Studies, University of Southern California. Prior to joining USC, he was director of the Marine Program at the Woodrow Wilson Center in Washington, D.C., permanent representative of Malta to the United Nations, ambassador of Malta to the United States, and a member of the United Nations Secretariat. Dr. Pardo is the author of numerous articles on the law of the sea, development, and disarmament.

LEIGH S. RATINER is a partner in the Washington, D.C., law firm of Dickstein, Shapiro & Morin. He has served as deputy chairman of the United States delegation to the Law of the Sea Conference during the Reagan administration, and has previously been a member of the United States delegation to that conference as a senior negotiator for the Departments of Defense, Interior, Energy, and State. He is also the author of a number of articles on natural resources, national security, and the oceans.

JAMES K. SEBENIUS is assistant professor of Public Policy and Management at the Kennedy School of Government, Harvard University. He has been a personal assistant to the administrator of the National Ocean and Atmospheric Administration (1976–77), a member of the U.S. delegation to the Law of the Sea Conference, and a financial consultant to the MIT group that produced *A Cost Model of Deep Ocean Mining and Associated Regulatory Issues* (1978). He is the author of the forthcoming *Agreements and Disagreements: Negotiation Analysis and the Law of the Sea* and numerous articles on negotiation, resource development, and public management.

INDEX